Praise for *Teaching Creati*

This book can teach us all how to think more effectively.

>Arthur L. Costa, Professor Emeritus, California State University,
>Co-Director, International Institute for Habits of Mind

This commendable new book charts a course for developing employees who are both inquisitive and collaborative in the classroom and beyond.

>John Cridland, Chairman, Transport for the North, former Director General, CBI

A hugely welcome book, full of practical examples of pedagogy to cultivate knowledge, skills and capabilities, all the while recognising the power of professional learning communities within and between schools.

>Dame Alison Peacock, Chief Executive, Chartered College of Teaching

The work Bill Lucas and his team are doing in examining the place of capabilities in the curriculum – and, perhaps more importantly, how to assess capabilities – is of critical importance.

>Dr David Howes, CEO, Victorian Curriculum and Assessment Authority

An intelligent, strongly evidenced and globally connected approach to developing creative thinkers in schools today.

>Matthew Taylor, Chief Executive, RSA

There is a risk in today's data-driven educational environment that knowledge and skill are emphasised at the expense of creative thinking. *Teaching Creative Thinking* shows us that this need not be the case; creativity can be embedded in all schools.

>Walter Boyle, Head Master, Holyport College

This book resonates strongly with the profession because it puts forward a powerful argument for scaffolding curriculum content through capabilities.

>Christine Cawsey, Principal, Rooty Hill High School, Sydney

If you still need convincing why your school or school system should prioritise critical thinking, look no further than *Teaching Creative Thinking*.

>Louise Stoll, Professor of Professional Learning, UCL Institute of Education

This powerful book gives a clear explanation of how and why creativity breathes life into the curriculum. Step away from the spreadsheets and read it!

Carolyn Roberts, Head Teacher, Thomas Tallis School

A must-read for educators and other professionals who are passionate about encouraging children and young people's critical and creative thinking.

Dr Leslie Gutman, Senior Lecturer and Programme Director, UCL Centre for Behaviour Change

Bill Lucas and Ellen Spencer's *Teaching Creative Thinking* is a must-read for anyone teaching in Scotland.

George Roberts, Head Teacher, Danestone Primary School and Heathryburn Primary School

Here is a book that creates the thrust for better learning in schools. It should be read by parents, teachers, learners, employers and policy-makers.

Mick Waters, Professor of Education, Wolverhampton University

At last, an approach to developing creativity in schools which eschews the false dualism of knowledge and skills in favour of a holistic approach to cultivating young people's capabilities.

Alex Crossman, Head Teacher, The Charter School East Dulwich

Lucas and Spencer provide the right mix of pedagogical and school practices, and real-life examples. Their framework will inspire a variety of readers, including teachers, school leaders and policy-makers.

Stéphan Vincent-Lancrin, Senior Analyst, OECD

This is a practical handbook, a resource to support far-reaching and high-impact developments, whose purpose is to raise standards and prepare young people for further learning and for life as high-functioning contributors to the workforce and to wider society.

Bill Watkin, Chief Executive, Sixth Form Colleges Association

Hats off to Bill Lucas and Ellen Spencer for *Teaching Creative Thinking* – a compelling case for capability-based education.

Keith Budge, Headmaster, Bedales Schools

Creativity in the classroom will not happen by accident, and this book gives valuable insights into how schools can promote it.

James Townsend, Director, The Church of England Foundation for Educational Leadership

Wholehearted thanks to Bill Lucas and Ellen Spencer for this hugely important book on the future of teaching.

Rhys Morgan, Director of Education, Royal Academy of Engineering

Today's employers tell us they need character, resilience, problem-solving and creativity in potential employees. Let's just get on with cultivating and valuing creative thinking as this book seeks to do.

Kirstie Donnelly, Managing Director, City & Guilds

Teaching Creative Thinking is a timely book, both expert and readable, which makes an authoritative case for the relevance of creative thinking to schools today.

Jonnie Noakes, Director,
Tony Little Centre for Innovation and Research in Learning, Eton College

Being able to think creatively opens the door to opportunity and this book brings a welcome global breadth to this vital topic.

Tony Little, Chief Academic Officer, GEMS Education

Pedagogy for a Changing World

Teaching Creative Thinking

Developing learners who generate ideas and can think critically

Bill Lucas and Ellen Spencer

Crown House Publishing Limited
www.crownhouse.co.uk

First published by

Crown House Publishing Limited
Crown Buildings, Bancyfelin, Carmarthen, Wales, SA33 5ND, UK
www.crownhouse.co.uk

and

Crown House Publishing Company LLC
PO Box 2223, Williston, VT 05495, USA
www.crownhousepublishing.com

© Bill Lucas and Ellen Spencer, 2017

The right of Bill Lucas and Ellen Spencer to be identified as the authors of this work has been asserted by them in accordance with the Copyright, Designs and Patents Act 1988.

First published 2017. Reprinted 2018.

All rights reserved. Except as permitted under current legislation no part of this work may be photocopied, stored in a retrieval system, published, performed in public, adapted, broadcast, transmitted, recorded or reproduced in any form or by any means, without the prior permission of the copyright owners. Enquiries should be addressed to Crown House Publishing.

Crown House Publishing has no responsibility for the persistence or accuracy of URLs for external or third-party websites referred to in this publication, and does not guarantee that any content on such websites is, or will remain, accurate or appropriate.

Extract pp. 154–155: adapted from 'What's worth knowing' from *Creative Schools: Revolutionizing Education from the Ground Up* by Ken Robinson and Lou Aronica © 2015, Ken Robinson. Used by permission of Viking Books, an imprint of Penguin Publishing Group, a division of Penguin Random House LLC. All rights reserved.

p. 104 Stuck poster © TLO
IFC, p. 121 and p. 179 © Rooty Hill High School
IBC, p. 127 and p. 164 © Thomas Tallis School
p. 177 © VCAA

British Library Cataloguing-in-Publication Data

Mindmaps are a trademark of the Buzan organisation.

A catalogue entry for this book is available from the British Library.

Print ISBN 978-178583236-9
Mobi ISBN 978-178583266-6
ePub ISBN 978-178583267-3
ePDF ISBN 978-178583268-0

LCCN 2017948774

Printed and bound in the UK by

TJ International, Padstow, Cornwall

Acknowledgements

Our huge thanks to:

Former and current colleagues at the Centre for Real-World Learning, Guy Claxton and Janet Hanson.

All those at the OECD who are exploring ways of teaching and assessing critical and creative thinking and with whom we have been in dialogue, especially Michael Stevenson and Stéphan Vincent-Lancrin and all of the teachers and educational leaders involved.

Our friends at the Mitchell Institute in Melbourne who have the cultivation of capabilities at their heart, especially Michelle Anderson, Stacey Fox, Sarah Glover, Peter Noonan, Megan O'Connell and Kate Torii.

All those at Victoria's education department and Curriculum and Assessment Authority, especially Lynn Davey, Sharon Foster, David Howes and all the schools with whom we have been prototyping approaches.

All the pioneering school leaders who have contributed case studies, including: Sarah Bergson, head teacher, Redlands Primary School; Ann Carter, head teacher, Duloe CE VA Junior and Infants School; Christine Cawsey, principal, Rooty Hill High School; Dianne Hennessy, former high school principal; Conny Mattimore, deputy principal, Rooty Hill High School; John Devlin, executive head teacher, Our Lady of Victories Primary School; Jill Howells, assistant principal, Brunswick East Primary School; Jon Nicholls, director of arts and creativity, Thomas Tallis School; and Carolyn Roberts, head teacher, Thomas Tallis School.

And Michael Fullan for great conversations along the way.

The authors and publisher would also like to thank:

- The Victorian Curriulum and Assessment Authority for permission to use a screenshot of their online assessment materials.

- The Organisation for Economic Co-operation and Development for permission to use the image OECD 2030 framework for education from *Global Competency for an Inclusive World*, page 2.
- Michael Fullan and colleagues for permission to use NPDL material.
- TLO for permission to use the Building Learning Power stuck poster text.

Contents

Acknowledgements i

Series Introduction: Capabilities and Pedagogy 1
    Changing roles for schools 1
    The purposes of education 3
    Which capabilities matter most? 5
    The idea of signature pedagogies 6
    A four-step process to cultivating capabilities in young people 9
    Learning to change 14
    About the series 15

Chapter 1: Creative Thinking 17
    A short history of creative thinking 17
    Creative thinking in more detail 23
    Why creative thinking matters today 28

Chapter 2: Cultivating Creative Thinkers 33
    Teaching for capability 33
    Five signature pedagogies 36
    The ecology of creative thinking 40
    Two core approaches 41
    Putting it all together in a school 43
    Focusing on the parts 46

Chapter 3: Getting Going 47
    Inquisitive 48
    Persistent 56

    Collaborative 65

    Disciplined 76

    Imaginative 84

Chapter 4: Going Deeper **95**

    Leadership for creative thinking 96

    Professional development for creative thinking 98

    Personal development and real-world learning 100

    Exploring signature pedagogies for cultivating creative thinking 102

    Engaging parents with the idea of creative thinking 110

    Co-curricular experiences for creative thinking 113

Chapter 5: Promising Practices **119**

    Rooty Hill High School, Sydney – leadership, visible thinking routines, professional learning and technology 120

    Thomas Tallis School, London – leadership, whole-school integration and pedagogy 126

    Redlands Primary School, Reading – growth mindsets, enquiry-based learning and the University of Redlands degree courses 130

    Brunswick East Primary School, Melbourne – multi-age learning communities, thinking routines and Philosophy for Children 134

    Our Lady of Victories Primary, Keighley – skills-led curriculum, sense of adventure and themed 'wonder weeks' 137

    Duloe Church of England School, Liskeard – creative cross-curricular connections and teachers supported to take risks 139

    OECD, France – PISA domains, understanding pedagogy and assessing progression in critical and creative thinking skills 144

Victorian Curriculum and Assessment Authority, Australia – support for schools to develop signature pedagogies and innovative approaches to assessment of capabilities 147

New Pedagogies for Deeper Learning, Canada – research based, clarity of progression within its defined capabilities and a commitment to pedagogies for building capabilities 150

Four Dimensional Education, USA – research based, clarity of progression within its defined competencies and an alliance of education leaders 152

Creative Schools 154

Educating Ruby and Building Learning Power, UK 156

Chapter 6: Signs of Success **159**

Pupils tracking progress 162

Teachers tracking progress 167

Real-world assessment options 173

Online assessment options 176

Chapter 7: Creative Challenges **181**

Appendix: An A–Z of Teaching and Learning Methods for Developing Creative Thinkers 191

References 197

Series Introduction

Capabilities and pedagogy

> Ensuring that all people have a solid foundation of knowledge and skills must therefore be the central aim of the post-2015 education agenda. This is not primarily about providing more people with more years of schooling; in fact, that's only the first step. It is most critically about making sure that individuals acquire a solid foundation of knowledge in key disciplines, that they develop creative, critical thinking and collaborative skills, and that they build character attributes, such as mindfulness, curiosity, courage and resilience.
>
> Andreas Schleicher and Qian Tang,
> *Universal Basic Skills: What Countries Stand to Gain* (2015, p. 9)

Changing roles for schools

Across the world there is a great shift taking place. Where once it was enough to know and do things, our uncertain world calls for some additional learning. We call them 'capabilities'. Others call them 'dispositions', 'habits of mind', 'attributes' or 'competencies', words we find very helpful. Some refer to them as 'non-cognitive skills', 'soft skills' or 'traits', none of which we like given, respectively, their negative connotations, tendency to belittle what is involved and association with genetic inheritance.

Our choice of capabilities is pragmatic. A country in the northern hemisphere like Scotland is actively using the term, as is Australia at the opposite end of the earth. If we had to choose a phrase to sum up our philosophy it would be 'dispositional teaching' – that is to say, the attempt specifically to cultivate in learners certain dispositions which evidence suggests are going to be valuable to them both at school and in later life.

We know that the shift is underway for four reasons:

1. One of the 'guardians' of global comparative standards, PISA, is moving this way. In 2012, as well as tests for 15-year-olds in English, maths and science, they introduced an 'innovative assessment domain' called 'creative problem-solving'. This became 'collaborative problem-solving' in 2015 and will become 'global competence' in 2018. 2021's assessment domain is 'creative thinking'.[1]

2. Researchers the world over are beginning to agree on the kinds of capabilities which do, and will, serve children well at school and in the real world. We'll explore this increasingly consensual list later on, but for now we want to share just some of the key thinkers to reassure you that you are in good company: Ron Berger, Guy Claxton, Art Costa, Anna Craft, Angela Duckworth, Carol Dweck, K. Anders Ericsson, Chris Fadel, Michael Fullan, Howard Gardner, Leslie Gutman, Andy Hargreaves, John Hattie, James Heckman, Lois Hetland, Bena Kallick, Tim Kautz, Geoff Masters, David Perkins, Lauren Resnick, Ron Ritchhart, Sir Ken Robinson, Andreas Schleicher, Ingrid Schoon, Martin Seligman, Robert Sternberg, Louise Stoll, Matthew Taylor, Paul Tough, Bernie Trilling, Chris Watkins, Dylan Wiliam and David Yeager. We'd include our own work in this field too.

3. Organisations and well-evidenced frameworks are beginning to find common cause with the idea of capabilities. The Assessment and Teaching of 21st Century Skills project, Building Learning Power, the Expeditionary Learning Network, the Global Cities Education Network, Habits of Mind, New Pedagogies for Deeper Learning, Partnership for 21st Century Learning and the Skills4Success Framework are just a few examples. We'd include our own Expansive Education Network in this too.

4. Inspirational leaders across the world are very gradually showing us that you can powerfully embed capabilities into the formal, informal and hidden curriculum of schools, if you have a mind to do so. Here are five examples:

---

1 Every three years the Programme for International Student Assessment (PISA) undertakes a worldwide study for the Organisation for Economic Co-operation and Development (OECD) in member and non-member nations of 15-year-old school pupils' performance in mathematics, science, reading and in one other 'innovative domain'. With Jack Buckley, Bill Lucas is co-chair of the Strategic Advisory Group overseeing the development of the creative thinking test in 2021.

Col·legi Montserrat in Spain, Hellerup School in Denmark, School 21 and Thomas Tallis School in England and Rooty Hill High School in Australia. You'll doubtless have your own favourites to add in. We admire these schools and their courageous teachers. Throughout the series, we hope that their stories and our grounded practical advice will serve to ensure that hundreds of thousands of schools across the world see the value of systematically cultivating capabilities, *as well as* deep disciplinary knowledge and useful academic or practical skills.

Increasingly, 'character' is the word used to describe the cluster of capabilities which are useful in life, with a further clarification of the term 'performance character' suggesting those attributes which are associated with excellence in situations where performance is called upon – an academic test, examination, sports match or any extra-curricular activity in which concentrated demonstration of a skill is called for.

All this means that as well as ensuring, as Andreas Schleicher and Qian Tang put it in the quotation which begins this chapter, all young people develop a solid foundation of knowledge and skills while at school, they also need to acquire a set of important capabilities.

The purposes of education

Parents, educators and policy-makers alike have many hopes for the education of children and young people. But with so many ideas about what schooling might achieve, it is hard to reach any kind of consensus. Nevertheless, in late 2015, the UK parliament initiated an inquiry into the 'purpose of education'. On the one hand, it is a telling admission if a government has to ask such a fundamental question. On the other, it could be construed as a sign of strength, as a recognition that times are changing.

At the Centre for Real-World Learning, we worked with a number of national bodies to see if common agreement could be reached. The list below is what we came up with, and it is indicative of the sorts of things we might all wish for our children's education to achieve (Lucas and Spencer, 2016). The first half a dozen are particularly relevant to this series of books, but the remainder also give a sense of our values. We want educational goals which:

1. Work for all young people.
2. Prepare students for a lifetime of learning at the same time as seeing childhood and school as valuable in their own right.
3. See capabilities and character as equally important as success in individual subjects.
4. Make vocational and academic routes equally valued.
5. Cultivate happier children.
6. Engage effectively with parents.
7. Engage well with business.
8. Use the best possible teaching and learning methods.
9. Understand how testing is best used to improve outcomes.
10. Empower and value teachers' creativity and professionalism.
11. Proactively encourage both rigorous school self-improvement and appropriate external accountability.

Which capabilities matter most?

Let's look in more detail at the third item on our wish list: seeing capabilities and character as equally important as success in individual subjects. In the last decade, we have begun to understand with greater clarity those capabilities which are particularly useful. Here are two lists, the first from an economic perspective (Heckman and Kautz, 2013) and the second through the eyes of educational researchers (Gutman and Schoon, 2013). Both sets of researchers are attempting to describe those capabilities or, in some cases, transferable skills which will improve outcomes for individual learners and so for wider society.

Heckman and Kautz:	**Gutman and Schoon:**
Perseverance	Self-perception
Self-control	Motivation
Trust	Perseverance
Attentiveness	Self-control
Self-esteem and self-efficacy	Metacognitive strategies
Resilience to adversity	Social competencies
Openness to experience	Resilience and coping
Empathy	Creativity
Humility	
Tolerance of diverse opinions	
Engaging productively in society	

The striking thing about these lists, to us, is how similar they are. While we may want to interrogate the terms more closely, the general direction is clear. The demand side, from employers, is similar in its emphasis to that of the educational researchers. The Confederation of British Industry launched a campaign setting out the kinds of capabilities it wanted young people to acquire at school. Their list included: grit, resilience, curiosity, enthusiasm and zest, gratitude, confidence and ambition, creativity, humility, respect and good manners, and sensitivity to global concerns (CBI, 2012).

The idea of signature pedagogies

If we are reaching consensus as to the kinds of capabilities increasingly being seen as valuable, what about the kinds of teaching and learning methods that might cultivate them? Is there a similar level of agreement? In truth, there is probably less so, mainly because, regardless of subject matter, there are some deeply engrained pre-perceptions. Teaching authoritatively from the front, for example, is something that those who see themselves as 'traditionalists' might advocate, but that most people would agree is only one kind of good teaching. By contrast, those who see themselves as more 'progressive' would argue that good teachers should be much less visible and their pupils engaged in self-organised group activities, another potentially good kind of more facilitative teaching.

We'd like to urge you not to adopt either of these binary positions, but instead to ask yourself some different questions:

- If I wanted to teach a pupil how to become more creative and better able to solve problems, what methods would I choose?
- If I wanted my students to become more resilient, what methods would I choose?
- If I wanted my pupils to be full of zest for learning, what methods would I choose?

Before you answer, we need to introduce you to an important concept – the idea of *signature pedagogies*. First suggested by Lee Shulman in the context of preparing learners for different vocational routes, these are 'the types of teaching that organize the fundamental ways in which future practitioners are educated for their new professions' (Shulman, 2005, p. 52). Shulman talks of the three dimensions of a signature pedagogy:

1. Its surface structure: 'concrete, operational acts of teaching and learning, of showing and demonstrating, of questioning and answering, of interacting and withholding, of approaching and withdrawing' (ibid., pp. 54–55).

2. Its deep structure: 'a set of assumptions of how best to impart a certain body of knowledge and know-how' (ibid., p. 55).

3. Its implicit structure: 'a moral dimension that comprises a set of beliefs about professional attitudes, values, and dispositions' (ibid., p. 55).

It's not much of a leap to think not about the fundamentals of a particular profession but instead of a particular capability. Suppose it were perseverance: how would you model and demonstrate it? What know-how does someone who is a good perseverer show, and how can you impart the clues of persevering to pupils? What are the underpinning self-belief and can-do dispositions that reinforce perseverance? Quite soon you are getting under the skin of a target capability. You begin to realise that some methods – having tactics for getting unstuck, asking for help, self-talk to keep going when others have given up – might be what you need to focus on.

Signature pedagogies are the teaching and learning methods which are most likely to lead to the desired capability and, throughout the series, we will be exploring these. In our earlier book, *Expansive Education: Teaching Learners for the Real World* (Lucas et al., 2013a), we introduced a ten-dimensional framework to help teachers think more carefully about the kinds of teaching and learning methods they might select. To do this, we encouraged them to reflect more about the kinds of outcomes they desired. Each line of our dimensions then serves as a prompt to think about learning methods suited to the desired outcome or outcomes and matched to a specific context.

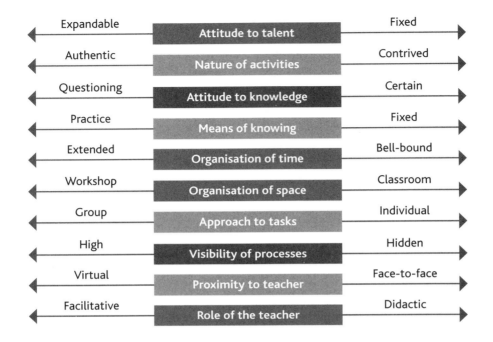

A ten-dimensional framework of pedagogical choices

Source: Lucas et al. (2013a, p. 136)

In some cases (e.g. our attitude to talent and the visibility of processes), we have powerful research evidence from Carol Dweck (2006) and John Hattie (2009) which means that we are always likely to choose methods which put us at the left of the continuum whatever we are teaching. But in others (e.g. means of knowing, approach to tasks and role of the teacher), decisions are likely to depend on the nature of the task, the timing within a lesson and the desired outcome. Take 'means of knowing' as an example and it becomes clear that in most situations teachers will want learners to be confident in both theory and practice. The question is really one of timing. Do you tell children that there is something called Ohm's law before you encourage them to play around with different ways of assembling electrical circuits, or do you let them discover the properties of voltage and current more experimentally before explaining that they are not the first to have noticed some important relationships between the two? The teacher decides.

The more a teacher moves from an 'instruction' approach to teaching, to what Chris Watkins (2005, p. 13) calls a 'co-construction' or more facilitative approach, the more decisions about the use of time, space and tasks look different and the more the role of the teacher changes. 'Good' teaching is an effective blend of the methods which are most likely to achieve desired outcomes. Typically these are a blend of capabilities, skills and knowledge.

A four-step process to cultivating capabilities in young people

From work with teachers across the world, and from the kinds of initiatives listed earlier in this introduction, there is a considerable amount known about how best to develop the kinds of capabilities at the core of performance character. Essentially it is a four-step process:

Step 1: Understand the capabilities

As well as being subject matter and skill experts, teachers have a vital third role: cultivating capabilities. Just as decisions have to be made about whether the timetable has scope to fit in both French and Spanish, so schools will want to decide which capabilities are most critical to them and on which they are going to focus. In some cases these will be value judgements and in others it will require a careful study of the research. Each book in the Pedagogy for a Changing World series takes a core capability and tries to get underneath its skin.

Step 2: Establish the classroom climate

Across the world much effort is expended in determining curriculum content. Governments rightly have a role in determining the kind of education their nation's children will receive, ensuring their chosen blend of competitive advantage,

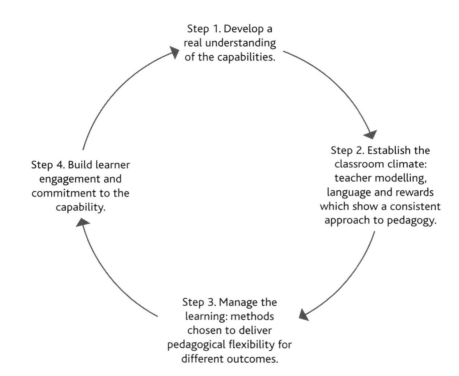

A four-step process of cultivating capabilities

Source: Centre for Real-World Learning

prosperity, social cohesion and well-being. As part of the process of qualifying to be a teacher, individuals demonstrate knowledge and understanding of one or more disciplinary areas. But at least as important as subject matter knowledge is pedagogical knowledge and skill (Coe et al., 2014). Teachers make thousands of decisions every day about the *process* of helping learners to learn. These kinds of pedagogical decisions are what we are concerned with in steps 2 and 3.

Creating the classroom climate, or culture, is about designing an environment that consistently communicates the right messages to learners, parents and teaching and support staff, both explicitly and implicitly. Each of these stakeholders will witness the extent to which capabilities are valued, or not, whether verbally or through what they see and experience. A classroom whose climate is conducive to the valuing and learning of capabilities will be distinctly to the left of our ten-dimensional model.

The way knowledge is acquired can be done in a way that closes off questioning or that helps learners to understand how we come to know certain facts. In science, for example, are learners taught theories as 'fact', or do they understand the limits of scientific theory and what makes a theory scientific? Do they understand the role of perspective or motive? Who wrote history? What was the worldview of our scientists? How do we know that? Why is it important? How can that thought process be used elsewhere?

Displays of work reflect what is valued. Where capabilities are valued, this might be shown in a visual demonstration of the process learners have been through of drafting and improving for excellence. Important as excellence in a final product is, we need to show and teach the process of getting there. A sense of crafting for improving is shown through displays of risk-taking and creativity that have led to failed attempts accompanied by thoughtful evaluations.

A whole host of capabilities – resourcefulness, curiosity, collaboration and critical thinking, for example – can be strengthened by access to appropriate resources as learners decide they are needed, as well as through the process of having to work out what tools might be required to complete a task.

Effective pedagogy will *always* involve the teacher modelling the capabilities they value. This includes a willingness to take risks, to collaborate with colleagues, to question their own understanding and their own readiness to learn.

Parents have an important role in supporting the messages teachers convey to learners about learning. They can either reinforce the capabilities at home or contradict them. In this respect, the education and involvement of parents is key.

Classroom systems of reward, recognition and sanction will need to align with any desired capabilities. Learners need to receive their teacher's commendation for the critical thinking behind a good essay.

Step 3: Manage the learning

Given that capabilities are not generally taught in a vacuum (although it is possible that a teacher might wish to focus on them aside from the lesson content – for example, in a school assembly), a fundamental management issue is the way that teachers ensure that learners value knowledge and skills at the same time as understanding the importance of developing their capabilities as learners in every lesson they experience.

Whether within the formal curriculum or outside it, it is important to name the capability explicitly: 'Today we're going to learn how to pass accurately, and I'd like all of you to see how many times you can practise this – *get your teammate to make it trickier each time so you are stretched to get better*.' In this example we are learning to throw a ball *and* we are learning about the importance of pushing ourselves.

In lessons, we know that certain approaches to teaching and learning work better than others. These include – when done rigorously – problem-based enquiry-led learning; Philosophy for Children approaches; the use of thinking routines, extended tasks and case studies; role play; and peer teaching, coaching and self-managed projects.

For learners, there are some core techniques which need to be mastered, just as they will need to become comfortable in their times tables, irregular verbs or acids and bases. These include:

- Giving and receiving feedback.
- Practising deliberately.
- Drafting and prototyping.
- Using design processes.
- Goal-setting.
- Mentally rehearsing.
- Verbalising the processes of learning.
- Reflecting on processes and progress.
- Self-testing.
- Working in groups.
- Teaching others.

In each of the books in this series, we will explore these techniques as and when they work well in different contexts.

Step 4: Build learner engagement

Schools which really embed capabilities rapidly realise that, for it to be sustainable and authentic, they need to be creative in engaging children and young people, giving them new roles, creating new co-curricular opportunities and partnering with a range of youth and community groups outside of the formal sector.

Within a primary class, this might take the form of asking children to take on the role of being question-noticer – listening carefully to the kind of questions being asked in a lesson and taking a moment at the end of the session to tell the class which one seemed the most effective and why. Secondary schools might like to invite a group of students, with support, to prepare a short demonstration lesson to present to their parents to show how their school is teaching all learners to develop as critical thinkers.

While we have described these four steps as if they are a simple linear progression, in practice it tends to be messier than this in the busy real world of schools. For example, using a particular pedagogy may lead to deeper understanding of a capability rather than the other way round.

Learning to change

Deliberately seeking to cultivate capabilities is hard because it involves change on multiple levels and cooperation from those around you. Change in education is particularly hard because of the complexity of school culture, the drive for 'performativity', the churn of sometimes unwelcome government initiatives and the tendency for politicians to oversimplify issues.

Changing habits that have become deeply engrained is harder still and requires sustained effort and support. However, habit formation is a slow, incremental process and habitual behaviour is very resistant to change. As well as using the ideas in this book, exploring the suggested resources and following up by looking at the websites of some of the case studies, we suggest that you connect with other like-minded colleagues.

You could start within your own school and then move outside to create a professional learning community, either locally or as part of a wider group such as the Expansive Education Network.[2] Professional learning communities within and between schools provide opportunities for teachers to take risks in a supportive environment and contribute significantly to the effective sharing of practice and ideas (Davies et al., 2013, p. 88).

---

2   See www.expansiveeducation.net.

Series Introduction

About the series

The Pedagogy for a Changing World series is action oriented and research led. The books are guides for teachers and school leaders who want to introduce and/or embed capabilities in their schools. Each book will offer practical suggestions as to how key capabilities can best be developed in learners, building both theoretical and practical confidence in the kinds of pedagogies which work well. The books are aimed at both primary and secondary levels.

The first three in the series are:

1. *Teaching Creative Thinking: Developing learners who generate ideas and can think critically*

2. *Developing Tenacity: Creating learners who persevere in the face of difficulty*

3. *Zest for Learning: Developing curious learners who relish real-world challenges*

Each book is structured in the following way:

- A clear definition of the capability and why it matters.
- An overview of pedagogies for cultivating the capability.
- Practical examples for getting started.
- More extended illustrations and descriptions of approaches.
- Promising practices – case studies of schools which are adopting these approaches.
- Challenges – a reminder of some of the pitfalls and how to overcome them.
- Suggestions as to how learners' progress can be tracked.

Chapter 1
Creative Thinking

What it is and why it matters

'There is no use trying,' said Alice. 'One *can't* believe impossible things.'

'I daresay you haven't had much practice,' said the Queen. 'When I was your age, I always did it for half-an-hour a day. Why, sometimes I've believed as many as six impossible things before breakfast.'

Lewis Carroll, *Through the Looking Glass, and What Alice Found There* (1872, p. 100)

In this chapter we offer a definition of creative thinking. We demonstrate that this capability has a long history, is highly relevant today and needs to be at the heart of the formal and informal experiences of school. As Lewis Carroll implies through the mouthpiece of the Queen in *Through the Looking Glass*, it can, like using imagination, be practised.

A short history of creative thinking

Creative thinking is what you do when you are being creative and creativity is the outcome of this. Creative activity is purposeful and generates something which is to some degree original and of value. Creative thinking is almost always a social activity and almost always takes place in response to an issue or problem facing an individual or group.

The study of creativity is some seventy years old. Most researchers trace its beginnings to the work of J. P. Guilford in the middle of the last century. Guilford (1950) suggested that there are two kinds of thinking: convergent (coming up with one good idea) and divergent (generating multiple solutions). In an English lesson, for example, a convergent response to the title 'The End of the World' might be to focus on a post-nuclear disaster, while a divergent approach might take any number of scenarios – terrorism, global warming, invasion by Martians and so forth – as its starting points. Building on this line of thought, E. Paul Torrance (1970) developed four sub-categories: fluency, flexibility, originality and elaboration. Each of these might be applied in our example as an indication of the degree of creative thinking being employed.

More recently, Robert Sternberg (1996) has argued that creativity is three dimensional. It requires synthesising (the ability to see problems in new ways and escape from conventional thinking), analysing (being able to recognise which ideas are worth pursing and which are not) and contextualising (having the skills in different settings to persuade others of the value of any specific idea).

Of course, creative thinking is both a solo and a collective activity and most often has a social component. Creativity can be viewed as domain-specific (e.g. being creative in science) or domain-free (being creative in any situation). Anna Craft reminds us that while only a few may aspire to be an exceptional genius, all of us can show a more ordinary form of creative thinking – what she termed 'little c creativity' (2001b). This book is full of suggestions to help teachers and their pupils to grow their little c creativity.

Donald Treffinger (Treffinger et al., 2002) found 120 definitions of creativity and helpfully grouped them into four broad categories: generating ideas, digging deeper into ideas, openness and courage to explore ideas, and listening to one's inner voice. We'll touch on each of these four ideas in this book. Sir Ken Robinson's celebrated TED talk, 'Do Schools Kill Creativity?' (2006), has helped to bring global interest to this topic and challenged us all to think about the way that schools are too often organised *not* to develop creative thinkers.

Two aspects of creative thinking have received increasing attention over the last decade: *problem-solving* and *critical thinking*.

When the respected international testing body PISA decided to explore collaborative problem-solving in 2015, this aspect of creative thinking received a significant boost (OECD, 2013). PISA argued that there was growing interest across the world in enquiry-based and problem-led learning, that employers valued the capability to solve problems and that such capabilities were so important that we should try to assess them. Various countries across the world (Singapore and Australia are just two examples) have begun to reflect this kind of thinking in their national curricula. Along with English, maths and science, creative problem-solving is increasingly being held up as a core part of what schools should be teaching.

The table below shows how PISA broke down collaborative problem-solving into its component elements. Along the top you can see the three main elements of collaborative problem-solving and down the left-hand side how these might be developed over time.

Matrix of collaborative problem-solving skills

	Establishing and maintaining shared understanding	Taking appropriate action to solve the problem	Establishing and maintaining team organisation
Exploring and understanding	Discovering perspectives and abilities of team members	Discovering the type of collaborative interaction to solve the problem, along with goals	Understanding roles to solve the problem
Representing and formulating	Building a shared representation and negotiating the meaning of the problem (common ground)	Identifying and describing tasks to be completed	Describing roles and team organisation (communication protocol/rules of engagement)

	Establishing and maintaining shared understanding	Taking appropriate action to solve the problem	Establishing and maintaining team organisation
Planning and executing	Communicating with team members about the actions to be/being performed	Enacting plans	Following rules of engagement (e.g. prompting other team members to perform their tasks)
Monitoring and reflecting	Monitoring and repairing the shared understanding	Monitoring results of actions and evaluating success in solving the problem	Monitoring, providing feedback and adapting the team organisation and roles

Source: OECD (2013, p. 11)

Collaborative problem-solving, as its name suggests, recognises that this activity has both a social component and a set of cognitive and non-cognitive skills useful for solving problems.

Critical thinking has been gaining in importance too. Its roots go back to Socrates and his approach to probing questioning. In Europe, the works of Francis Bacon (*Of the Proficience and Advancement of Learning, Divine and Human*, 1605) and René Descartes (*Rules for the Direction of the Mind*, 1701) laid out the foundations for an approach to thinking that is systematic and disciplined – the foundations of what we would today think of as scientific enquiry.

In the last century, John Dewey argued that critical (or what he called 'reflective') thinking was at the heart of education. He defined it as: 'Active, persistent, and careful consideration of a belief or supposed form of knowledge in the light of the grounds that support it, and the further conclusions to which it tends' (Dewey, 1910, p. 6).

In the 1990s and early twenty-first century there has been renewed interest in 'good thinking', as evidenced in initiatives such as thinking skills, thinking routines and Philosophy for Children. In the United States, Art Costa and Bena Kallick (2000) developed a set of sixteen habits of mind to describe the attributes of intelligent thinkers. These include a number of critical thinking habits such as 'thinking about thinking', 'questioning and posing problems', 'applying past knowledge to new situations', 'thinking and communicating with clarity and precision', 'creating, imagining, innovating', 'taking responsible risks' and 'thinking interdependently'.

In the UK, there was a period when each of the four home nations had personal learning and thinking skills (PLTS) as a desired focus of schooling. These were a set of six skill clusters – independent enquirers, effective participants, reflective learners, team workers, self-managers and creative thinkers. But they were always advisory and not mandatory and often got lost when set alongside subjects in which children were tested and examined.

In Australia, the Melbourne Declaration of 2008 explicitly laid out a goal that 'all young Australians become successful learners, confident and creative individuals, and active and informed citizens' (MCEETYA, 2008, p. 8). This aspiration has subsequently led to the creation of a capability-led curriculum in all Australian schools (ACARA, 2015) stressing the importance of, for example, critical and creative thinking.

The Partnership for 21st Century Skills (now Partnership for 21st Century Learning, or P21) is one of a number of groups suggesting that critical thinking is a key skill for students if they are to be properly prepared for post-secondary education and working life. They identify four key skills: reasoning effectively, using systems thinking, making judgements/decisions and solving problems.[1]

Most recently, the PISA board has agreed that the focus of its innovative domain test in 2021 will be creative thinking, and will draw on the five-dimensional model of creativity explored in this book and described in detail in the following pages.

---

1   See http://www.p21.org/our-work/p21-framework.

In this book, we have tried to bring these various traditions of thinking together by defining creativity and creative thinking in terms of five habits of mind (inquisitive, persistent, collaborative, disciplined and imaginative):

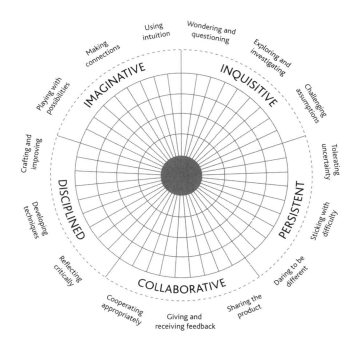

The Centre for Real-World Learning's five-dimensional model of creative thinking

Our definition is as much about the sciences or humanities as it is about the arts. It values both exploratory possibility thinking as well as focused analytical problem-solving. It sees creative thinking, or small c creativity, as something that can and should be learned at school. And as you will see from the activities in the book, it suggests that creative thinking can be taught and learned in classrooms, learned through the co-curriculum and picked up via the culture of schools and their communities.

Creative thinking in more detail

The five dimensions of creative thinking offer a broad view of creativity. Each is applicable to a range of real-world types of creative activity, from science to the performing arts. Most importantly, there is compelling evidence to suggest that they are all learnable. While the five habits are adjectives (e.g. imaginative) describing the person, the fifteen sub-habits are action phrases (like 'playing with possibilities') to ensure that the concepts are well grounded.

Two of the dimensions, disciplined and collaborative, are too often neglected in schools. Disciplined challenges the idea that creative ideas or products emerge instantly. It reminds us that learners need to spend time developing expertise and skill, all the while crafting and improving their work. For some people critical thinking is thought to be incompatible with creativity, but we will suggest ways in which it is very much part and parcel of being a creative thinker. Being creative is about creating something new *for a purpose*; it's not enough to come up with a hundred ways to make a process more efficient if you don't then choose one and implement it. You're not creative if your ideas are so far-fetched and ill thought through that they get shelved. We see creativity as the bigger category, requiring critical thinking.

Also undervalued in too many schools is the importance of collaborative learning. We would not, for example, have the world's first particle accelerator, the Large Hadron Collider at CERN, were it not for the extraordinary shared creativity of many people from a multitude of different disciplines. At a much more modest level, the same kind of thinking needs to occur in schools where it is all too easy just to focus assessment on the learning outcomes of individuals rather than on their ability to work creatively with others (something they will need throughout their working lives).

The five creative thinking habits break down in the following way.

Inquisitive

Creative individuals are good at uncovering and pursing interesting and worthwhile questions both in a specific subject and more generally.

- Wondering and questioning. Not simply curious, creative individuals pose concrete questions about things to help them understand and develop new ideas.

- Exploring and investigating. Questioning things alone does not make a creative thinker. Creative individuals act out their curiosity through exploration and follow up on their questions by actively seeking and finding out more.

- Challenging assumptions. It's important to maintain a degree of appropriate scepticism, not taking things at face value without critical examination.

An example of being inquisitive in a primary school might be starting a lesson by putting a battered suitcase with a range of clothes and other items in it on a desk in the middle of the classroom and inviting the pupils to speculate as to who the case's owner might have been and what he or she might have been doing.

An example of being inquisitive in a secondary school might be starting a science lesson by providing pupils with a choice of scientific instruments where similar items use different scales (e.g. a beaker with 10 ml as its smallest division and one with 50 ml divisions) and requiring them to justify their choice. If the opportunity is given to rerun the experiment with a better choice of scales, this helps to teach them that science is an iterative process.

Persistent

Creative individuals do not give up easily.

- Tolerating uncertainty. Being able to tolerate uncertainty is important when actions or even goals are not fully set out.

- Sticking with difficulty. Persistence in the form of tenacity is important, enabling an individual to get beyond familiar ideas and come up with new ones.

- Daring to be different. Creative thinking demands a certain level of self-confidence as a prerequisite for sensible risk-taking.

An example of being persistent in a primary school might be a classroom reward system which routinely features the gritty pupil of the week as part of a sustained focus on things which pupils can do when they get stuck in their work. The results could be displayed on the classroom wall.

An example of being persistent in a secondary school might be for a teacher to assign particular viewpoints or sides of an argument to pupils and then require them to debate the position, so developing the habit of developing and holding to a line of argument.[2]

Collaborative

In today's world complex challenges require creative collaboration. Creative individuals recognise the social dimension of the creative process.

- Sharing the product. Creative outputs matter, whether they are ideas or things creating impact beyond their creator.

- Giving and receiving feedback. Creative thinkers want to contribute to the ideas of others and hear how their own ideas might be improved.

- Cooperating appropriately. The creative individual cooperates with others, taking into account the nature of the group, the kind of problem and the stage which the group has reached.

---

[2] See, for example, The Noisy Classroom: http://noisyclassroom.com/video/how-to-prepare-for-a-debate.

An example of being collaborative in a primary school might be routinely teaching techniques for working in pairs (such as the think–pair–share technique) over a term and then developing a staff resource full of practical examples.

An example of being collaborative in a secondary school at Key Stage 3 might be taking a poem or ballad (Charles Causley's 'The Ballad of Charlotte Dymond' works well) and treating it as if it were a real-life incident, working in teams to create and act out (or film) interviews with key characters in the poem, all designed to shed light on what might actually have happened.

Disciplined

Like any subject, creative thinking requires knowledge and skill in crafting and shaping the creative product or process.

- Reflecting critically. Evaluation is the way in which progress can be seen and understood and the quality of new ideas or novel thinking can be checked.

- Developing techniques. Creative thinkers practise a range of conceptual and practical skills in order to improve.

- Crafting and improving. Taking pride in work, attending to details, practising and correcting any errors are indicators of the higher levels of creative thinking.

An example of being disciplined in a primary school might involve teaching pupils to make specific, descriptive comments on a piece of work by another pupil. The pupil is helped to see how he could make his work resemble the model he is aiming at more closely. He is then able to improve his work by redrafting.[3]

An example of being disciplined in a secondary school could involve a similar kind of group critique and take place in design and technology, art and design or almost any class where 'things' are being made. Timely pauses throughout a lesson allow

---

3 'Austin's Butterfly' is a well-known example that demonstrates the astounding potential of young children to take on board critique to produce top-quality work. See http://eleducation.org/resources/austins-butterfly.

students to regroup and comment on the progress of one another's work in ways which are kind, specific and practically useful.[4]

Imaginative

At the heart of creative thinking is the ability to come up with imaginative solutions and possibilities.

- Playing with possibilities. Developing an idea involves manipulating it, trying it out and improving it.

- Making connections. Seeing new links between ideas is an important aspect of the synthesising process of creative thinking.

- Using intuition. The use of intuition allows individuals to make new connections tacitly that would not necessarily materialise using analytical thinking alone.

An example of being imaginative in a primary school might be to stop a story at various stages of its development and invite the children to play with its possibilities, taking it in many different directions. You could do this with no guidance at all or introduce additional constraints (e.g. a sudden accident, a stranger arrives, you go blind).

An example of being imaginative in a secondary school might be for a class to take an event in history and think through what might have happened if different decisions had been taken. For example, what would have happened had the rescue at Dunkirk failed? What if Nazi Germany had won the Second World War? What if the English had won the Battle of Hastings?[5]

---

4 In an art and design context, a team from Harvard University's Project Zero explored how teaching of the arts imparts habits of mind to learners. See Hetland et al. (2007).
5 For examples of hypothetical historical scenarios see: https://www.quora.com/topic/Alternate-Histories-Hypothetical-Historical-Scenarios and http://brilliantmaps.com/what-if-nazi-germany-won-world-war-ii/.

Why creative thinking matters today

Knowledge is essential. Skills are important. Capabilities are vital. All are needed in the twenty-first century, when change is relatively rapid, the store of human knowledge is expanding faster than ever, work is increasingly international and problems ever more complex.

There is an argument made more and more – for example, by Sir Ken Robinson and the OECD's Andreas Schleicher – that creativity is a new literacy and should be regarded with the same status as English or maths. Whether you agree with this opinion or not, there are a number of different arguments which, taken together, make the case for creative thinking.

Here are just a few of them, starting with the individual perspective and moving outwards to a global one.

It improves outcomes for learners

Leslie Gutman and Ingrid Schoon (2013) recently reviewed the evidence and concluded that creativity, perseverance and various metacognitive strategies (which we have described in our model of creative thinking) improve outcomes for learners.

Various studies have shown the benefits of specific aspects of creative thinking, such as these three examples:

1. Curiosity and being inquisitive (Friedman, 2005)
2. Persistence, perseverance and grit (Duckworth et al., 2007)
3. Giving and receiving certain kinds of feedback (Hattie and Gan, 2011)

It's associated with improved well-being

Martin Seligman and Mihalyi Csikszentmihalyi (2000) make this case powerfully, and Csikszentmihalyi (1996, p. 344) sums it up delightfully:

> Personal creativity may not lead to fame and fortune, it can do something that from the individual's point of view is even more important: make day-to-day experiences more vivid, more enjoyable, and more rewarding. When we live creatively, boredom is banished and every moment holds the possibility of a fresh discovery.

It makes learners more employable

Organisations and businesses that thrive on innovation need people who think creatively and can solve problems. In the UK, the CBI have been campaigning for creativity and associated concepts, such as curiosity and resilience, being core outcomes of schooling (CBI, 2012). The recent World Economic Forum Global Challenge Insight Report (2016) is illustrative. Its top four desired cognitive abilities are cognitive flexibility, creativity, logical reasoning and problem sensitivity, along with a number of cross-functional skills. The Foundation for Young Australians analysed over four million job advertisements over the previous three years and observed which skills had the biggest increase in demand. Besides 'digital literacy' and presentation skills, the explicit demand for critical thinking skills had increased by 158% and creativity by 65% (Canny, 2016).

There's a strong economic case for its benefits

Nobel laureate James Heckman and his colleague Tim Kautz (2012) make these arguments very clearly and show how creative thinking habits are valued across the world.

It's increasingly tested and valued internationally

We have already shown how PISA has led thinking about collaborative problem-solving. The growing importance of the International Baccalaureate, the Partnership for 21st Century Learning, Building Learning Power and New Pedagogies for Deeper Learning provide further evidence of the growing influence of creative thinking.

It's increasingly required by national curricula

Australia, Finland, New Zealand, Scotland and Singapore are just five examples.

It's vital in a web-based world

The Internet has given us an overflowing water hydrant of information, opinions and misinformation. Wikipedia is both an asset and a challenge. Our ability to explore, challenge assumptions and reflect critically are crucial to our online sanity and effectiveness.

It's important in life

The modern world provides plenty of problems in need of creative solutions. It always did, of course; however, the world no longer rewards people for what they know, but for what they can do with that knowledge. Google, one of the world's most selective companies, is more interested in generalists who can learn than those with more traditional CVs with their subject grades (see Green, 2014). Of course, people have always had to think creatively to find solutions to problems, but in an age when change is that much faster and individuals are often expected to be 'experts' in multiple fields over the course of their lives, it assumes an even greater importance.

The lines of thought we have explored so far are just the tip of the iceberg. Doubtless you will have your own views. Indeed, one useful way of taking the whole concept of creative thinking into a staffroom or classroom is to start by posing a question: how do you currently think creatively in your life? Share examples of what you do when you are thinking most creatively. With younger pupils you may have to break down the abstract concept of creative thinking into smaller chunks, like the fifteen we have used in our model (see page 22). On the other hand, they may just surprise you!

Chapter 2
Cultivating Creative Thinkers

Signature pedagogies

> Creativity isn't a switch that's flicked on or off; it's a way of seeing, engaging and responding to the world around you.
>
> Rod Judkins, *The Art of Creative Thinking* (2015, pp. 6–7)

Let's go back to one of our questions in the introduction. If you wanted to teach someone how to become more creative and better able to solve problems, what methods would you choose? How, in short, could you help them to become creative thinkers?

In this chapter we will explore the pedagogies and teaching and learning methods that are most likely to cultivate young people who are creative thinkers.

Teaching for capability

Let's remind ourselves of the four-step process for cultivating any capability which we outlined in the introduction:

Step 1: Develop real understanding of the capability.

Step 2: Establish the classroom climate. Use of space/layout, teacher modelling, language and rewards which show a consistent approach to pedagogy.

Step 3: Manage the learning. Methods chosen to deliver pedagogical flexibility for different outcomes.

Step 4: Build learner engagement and commitment to the capability.

In this chapter we are going to be focusing on steps 2 and 3, and beginning to see some of the ways in which step 4 can be achieved.

Stop and think for a moment about a particular class or group of pupils that you know well. Now have another look at our five-dimensional model on page 22 and think specifically about some of the more concrete aspects of creative thinking – like questioning, sticking with difficulty or giving and receiving feedback, for example.

Reflect on how you currently teach these (if you do!). If you don't currently focus on them specifically, consider how you might introduce and teach a lesson or series of lessons in which, as well as whatever subject you are focusing on, you explicitly try to embed one of these skills too. We use the climate-related ideas of space, modelling, language and rewards and a range of method-focused ideas to think some of this through.

Let's suppose you are teaching science. How do you create a laboratory environment in which students ask really good questions and are deeply inquisitive? Or maybe it's an English lesson and you are pondering how to help a pupil write more fluently and more extensively in English, or to stick with the process of writing which they currently find challenging. Or perhaps you want maths students to share their workings on a difficult problem in pairs and give useful feedback to each other as to how they went about it.

For each of these three examples it is possible to use steps 2 and 3 as a mental prompt. What kind of classroom climate would be conducive? For instance, if you are trying to encourage students to work collaboratively on an agreed challenge, you may want the classroom laid out so that it is more like a workshop where they can get tools or materials as they need them (rather than a more traditional classroom where such things are in a cupboard to which you hold the key!).

How might you, as the teacher, model creative thinking? By breaking it down into its five habits you could address persistent, for example, as you demonstrate your willingness to grapple. As you try to make that new app work in class, what kind of language will be most helpful? We know that it is beneficial to learners if they can think of their progress as provisional and emergent, rather than inevitable or fixed. To this end, saying that you can't do something is unhelpful. Suggesting instead that you cannot *yet* work out how to do it is much more useful.

Let's take another habit: inquisitive. How might you show yourself to be an inquisitive learner when a student asks you a question to which you don't know the answer? Can you model to students how you think about what you *do* know in order to reason what the answer might be?

How will you reward success in achieving an aspect of creative thinking? Within a classroom it is perfectly possible to create your own internal currency for success in creative thinking. This could be as simple as explicitly noticing achievements ('Well done for sticking with that tricky sum, Jim') or as complex as a reward system for all aspects of creative thinking as used by one of our case study schools, Thomas Tallis (see Chapter 5).

Which teaching methods will you choose? Let's suppose you are trying to encourage better questioning, what methods would work best? Do you start a lesson by introducing a mystery item and inviting speculation about it? Do you begin with questions on a new topic which pupils have pre-prepared as part of their homework? Do you have a part of one of the classroom's walls already designated as a 'question wall' where interesting and tricky questions are regularly posted? Any one of these ideas would be a useful way of approaching the subject of questioning.

Many educators have pondered ways of promoting better questioning and enquiry. We particularly like the set of questions used by the International Baccalaureate Organization in their *IB Learner Profile Booklet*:

> Is it possible to create more experiences and opportunities in the classroom that allow students to be genuine inquirers?
>
> How could we give students more time to develop their ability to work effectively as a team?
>
> Could we create more opportunities to discuss the ethical issues that arise in the subjects we teach?

How well do we model empathy, compassion and respect for others in our classrooms and around the school?

Do our assessment strategies encourage critical and creative thinking?

How well do we report on individual students' development of the qualities in the Learner Profile?

How could we empower students to take more responsibility for their own learning? (adapted from International Baccalaureate Organization, 2008, pp. 3–5)

Paradoxically, it can sometimes be helpful to think how *not* to teach something. You would not, we imagine, expect pupils to develop strong questioning techniques if they never have a chance to practise these because they are always answering questions you have posed! Seeing things as starkly as this can help you to avoid missing obvious solutions.

Five signature pedagogies

As you mull over the different ways in which you might cultivate creative thinking capability, you will probably begin to appreciate (or remind yourself if you are already familiar with this kind of thought process) that certain kinds of teaching methods are much more likely to be effective than others.

This line of thought brings us back to the idea of signature pedagogies which we introduced in the introduction. Signature pedagogies are the kinds of learning methods most suited to a particular desired outcome. In this book we are focusing on creative thinking and so our desired outcomes are the fifteen aspects of this which we have already suggested. By 'signature' we mean those methods which are most closely associated with what we want to learn. Such methods are, if you like, the unique DNA or fingerprint of creative thinking. We will also refer to these as 'signature methods' and in this book we will be exploring many of them. (For ease of access we have also listed them alphabetically in the appendix.)

Five inter-connected pedagogies are of particular relevance to the cultivation of creative thinking:

1. Problem-based learning
2. Classroom learning community
3. Playful experimentation
4. Growth mindset
5. Deliberate practice

By *problem-based learning* we mean learning that starts with real-world problems and, through a rigorous process of enquiry, enables learners to conduct research – integrating both theory and practice – and apply their knowledge and skills to develop potential solutions. At the heart of this approach are design processes such as the ones described in the examples below.

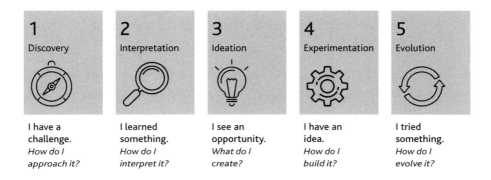

The five phases of the design process

Source: Adapted from http://www.designthinkingforeducators.com/design-thinking/

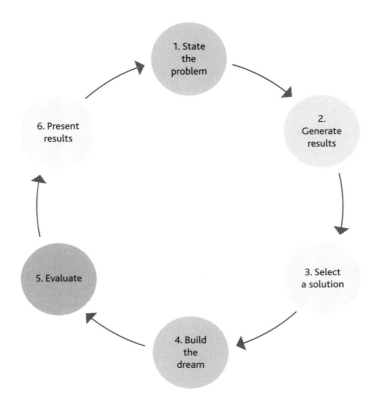

The engineering design process

Source: Adapted from https://mynasadata.larc.nasa.gov/engineering-design/

Problem-based learning approaches are a powerful way of developing inquisitive learners.

A *classroom learning community* describes an approach to teaching and learning which is deeply social, where the goal is to advance the collective knowledge of a class and so support the growth of their individual knowledge. In this we draw, in particular, on the work of Chris Watkins (2005) and colleagues at the University College London Institute of Education (IoE).

Classroom learning communities have five defining features:

1. Community forming. Getting to know each other; telling the story we bring appreciatively.

2. Community agenda. Eliciting the questions brought to the theme; helping learners to plan intentional learning.

3. Community activities for learning. Reciprocal teaching; development of dialogue; jigsaw tasks; meta-learning; group goals for assessment.

4. Community governance. Classroom reviews; shared control; 'the classroom we want'.

5. Community climate. Pro-social behaviour; development of trust; helping each other to learn; affiliation; not bonding but bridging.

Other research from the IoE and its partners, such as the Social Pedagogic Research into Group-work (SPRinG) project, is helpful in understanding the dynamics of successful group work in primary classrooms.[1]

These approaches are central to an understanding of collaborative working.

By *playful experimentation* we mean the conscious, often playful, and sometimes non-conscious generation of new ideas, as well as more explicit approaches to synthesising knowledge and experiences. Recently we have begun to refer to this kind of pedagogy as 'tinkering' (Lucas et al., 2017).

This kind of approach is important in the development of imagination.

Growth mindset, a term coined by Carol Dweck (2006), is strongly linked to another idea, 'grit' (Duckworth et al., 2007). Learners need to understand that their capacity for intelligent thinking and behaviour can grow as they practise things. We have created the phrase 'expansive education' to describe these kinds of approaches (Lucas et al., 2013a).

This approach is core to the development of persistent learners.

---

1 See www.spring-project.org.uk.

By *deliberate practice* we mean a series of highly structured activities, such as drafting, redrafting, prototyping and rehearsing, undertaken with the specific goal of improving performance. Deliberate practice involves a level of task motivation. The teacher must gauge the difficulty of the task requiring practice, and take into account pre-existing knowledge, skill or capability, so that the task can be correctly understood after just a brief period of instruction. It involves the provision of real-time feedback for learning and the repeated repetition of the same or similar tasks. In this we draw on the research of K. Anders Ericsson (2016).

This kind of rigorous focus on improving performance is essential to the development of any disciplined thinking or practice.

The ecology of creative thinking

As well as a set of sympathetic pedagogies, there are also some important environmental and cultural factors to consider whether considering primary or secondary schools. David Harrington (1990) has helpfully described the elements of a creative environment, which include:

- Opportunities for play, experimentation and exploration.
- Children feel comfortable in taking risks and making mistakes.
- Exciting or unusual contexts are often used for learning.
- Opportunities for free-flowing thinking and idea generation.
- Opportunities for critical reflection that is supportive and formative.
- Children encouraged to take ownership of their learning.
- Respect for difference and for others' creativity.
- Children able to make choices in terms of tasks and approaches.

It might be worth stopping for a moment to consider the ways in which your own classroom environment currently provides these kinds of opportunities and to reflect on where you might do even more to enhance your teaching and learning environment.

At the wider level, in a study undertaken for the European Commission (KEA, 2009), four key areas were shown to be important in developing effective creative learning environments: the physical environment needs to be stimulating, creative teaching methods need to be deployed, teachers need to be trained, and partnerships need to exist between schools and external bodies to stimulate creative thinking. Again, you may wish to reflect on the degree to which these four areas are well catered for in your school or schools.

Two core approaches

Whatever pedagogical approach you choose, and whatever environment you find yourself in, there are two important approaches which will be helpful – *split-screen teaching* and *visible thinking*. Both of these play an important role in making explicit connections between creative thinking and the world of disciplinary knowledge, by which most schools are organised and which appears on student timetables, and the need to make these kinds of linkages visible and routine.

Split-screen teaching invites teachers to describe two worlds, the disciplinary subject matter of their lesson and the capability on which they are also focusing. As part of the evolution of Building Learning Power, teachers have found it helpful to think explicitly about their teaching as having two 'screens.'[2] One screen is the knowledge and skills and the other is the capability. Let's say you were introducing a science activity to understand the properties of acids and bases, then pupils were to prepare a short demonstration for other pupils, who would in turn offer feedback to their peers on the effectiveness of their explanations. Or in a history lesson, students might be looking at the causes of the First World War at the same time as they are exploring aspects of critical thinking, such as the use of primary sources of evidence.

---

2 A good example of the split-screen teaching technique in practice can be found in Fawcett (2012).

In the imaginary split screen of the lesson and its objectives, a teacher would take care to explain to the class that both the chemistry (acids and bases) and the creative thinking (giving and receiving feedback) objectives were equally important.

The visible thinking approach, initiated by Harvard University's Project Zero, has identified a number of important 'thinking routines' which help pupils to develop capabilities such as creative thinking. As its website puts it:

> Routines exist in all classrooms; they are the patterns by which we operate and go about the job of learning and working together in a classroom environment. A routine can be thought of as any procedure, process, or pattern of action that is used repeatedly to manage and facilitate the accomplishment of specific goals or tasks. Classrooms have routines that serve to manage student behavior and interactions, to organizing the work of learning, and to establish rules for communication and discourse. Classrooms also have routines that structure the way students go about the process of learning.[3]

In this book we are most interested in the kinds of routines which make explicit connections between knowledge domains — science, history, art, for example — and the fifteen aspects of creative thinking which we are exploring. There are some core routines which work well, of which these are three examples:

1. What makes you say that? Students are asked to describe something, such as an object or concept, and then support their interpretation with evidence; an interpretation with justification routine.

2. Think–puzzle–explore: Students are invited to think, then puzzle, then explore ideas when they are beginning a topic to help develop their own questions to investigate; a routine that sets the stage for deeper enquiry.

3. Think–pair–share: Students are encouraged to think about something, such as a problem, question or topic, and then articulate their thoughts; a routine for active reasoning and explanation.

Indeed, a good number of Project Zero's thinking routines will be relevant for introducing topics with an explicit focus on the five creative thinking habits.

---

3   See http://www.visiblethinkingpz.org/VisibleThinking_html_files/03_ThinkingRoutines/03a_ThinkingRoutines.html.

Teachers may wish to incorporate these into their repertoire in addition to the 'starter' activities we suggest in Chapter 3.

Putting it all together in a school

So far, we have been exploring some important pedagogical principles for developing capabilities such as creative thinking, and taking a moment to consider the features of the learning environment which are likely to be most conducive. By way of rounding this off, remember that creative thinking needs a cohesive and consistent approach, as David Perkins and Robert Duron remind us.

Play the whole game

David Perkins (2009) talks of the 'whole game of learning'. Long concerned with providing students with richly engaging, rigorous and relevant learning experiences, Perkins uses the 'whole game' as a metaphor to describe the kinds of holistic education we need to be providing to young people which will be useful to them in their later lives. Specifically, he is interested in developing learners who are resourceful and able to transfer their learning from one context to another. His seven simple pieces of advice, drawing from some four decades of research, still seem to us highly relevant and useful. The first phrase in each item are the exact words Perkins uses, the remaining words are our own adaptation to the topic of creative thinking.

- Play the whole game. Use extended projects and authentic contexts so that learners are less likely to be thrown when they encounter something new.

- Make the game worth playing. Work hard at engaging learners, giving them choices wherever possible, and so build the range of self-control strategies they need.

- Work on the hard parts. Discover the most effective ways of practising so that making mistakes and learning from them becomes normal resourceful behaviour.

- Play out of town. Try things out in many different contexts so that even if something seems slightly different, the learners have more confidence to persist.

- Uncover the hidden game. Make the processes of learning as visible as possible so that students, teachers and other adult helpers have a common language to set goals and chart progress.

- Learn from the team and the other teams. Develop robust ways of working in groups and seek out relevant learning communities so that when learners encounter novel situations they have already learned how to use the resources of those around them.

- Learn from the game of learning. Be in the driving seat as a learner, developing tried and tested tactics and strategies which are regularly practised.

You might like to think about the ways in which you are (or are not yet) playing the whole game of creative learning in your school.

Planning your lessons to build in critical thinking

Developed by Robert Duron and colleagues (2006) we think this model may be useful to teachers thinking about teaching and learning.

Their five-step process encourages teachers to conduct lesson planning beginning with the desired learning objective in mind.

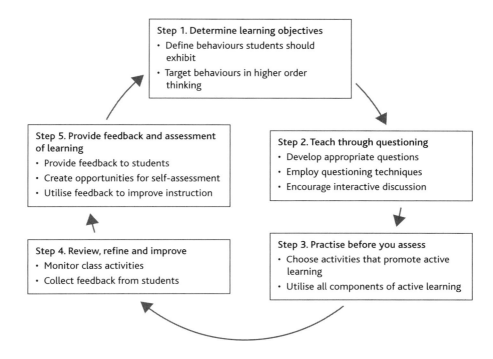

Five-step model to move students towards critical thinking

Source: Duron et al. (2006, p. 161)

You might like to use this approach as part of your school's or team's professional development to reflect on an aspect of creative thinking that you are about to plan. You could start by selecting which of the fifteen sub-habits of the creative thinking model you are interested in and which subjects seem to be the best context for their development.

Focusing on the parts

As well as the bigger picture, it is also important to start small and focus on some specific signature methods for cultivating creative thinking capabilities.

In the next chapter, we look in more detail at each of the five creative thinking habits, offer some more specific tried and tested methods, and suggest ways in which you might start out a lesson or sequence of lessons exploring an aspect of creative thinking.

Chapter 3
Getting Going

Some suggestions for starting out

> Odd how the creative power at once brings the whole universe to order. I can see the day whole, proportioned – even after a long flutter of the brain such as I've had this morning[;] it must be a physical, moral, mental necessity, like setting the engine off.
>
> Virginia Woolf, *A Writer's Diary* (2012, p. 213)

In this chapter, we look at ways of engaging more specifically with each of our fifteen aspects of creative thinking. By 'starting out' we mean two things. First of all, we imagine a teacher might wish to stop and reflect on ways of cultivating creative thinking as they break down a broad scheme of work into more detailed lesson plans, with activities as part of the subject they are teaching.

Second, we have in mind the literal association with starting out a lesson: the starter. For a period of time, teachers followed a fairly rigid structure of starter, learning objective, main activity and review or plenary activity. These days, most teachers have rightly become more flexible and nuanced in their interpretation of these kinds of processes, although many still find the idea of a starter activity a useful one. It can be an effective way of grabbing pupils' attention and, when well chosen, of setting the tone for the rest of a lesson or series of lessons.

In the figure on page 49, we show the five broad signature pedagogies associated with creative thinking which we discussed in the previous chapter, along with a suggested approach to teaching and learning methods that might work for each sub-habit.

Our model should start to help you get your own head around the complexities underpinning the concept of creative thinking and give you some ideas to stimulate your lesson planning.

As you think about getting started (or restarted if you are already underway) it will be helpful to bear in mind our earlier four-step plan:

1. How will you develop real understanding of each of the five dimensions of creative thinking?
2. How will you establish the classroom climate in which your selected dimension or dimensions will flourish?
3. Which methods will work best to cultivate your selected dimension or dimensions?
4. How will you build learner engagement?

In this chapter we take each of our five dimensions in turn, making some general remarks about their essential features, exploring one of our five suggested signature pedagogies and suggesting a core approach and some starter ideas for each of the three sub-habits.

Inquisitive

Being curious and inquisitive is at the heart of what it is to be an effective learner and is central to creative thinking. It is all too easy in teaching to assume that inquisitiveness is a one-way street; a set of questions by a teacher requiring answers by learners. Creative thinking classrooms value pupils' inquisitiveness at least as much. It is an exciting moment, for example, when a learner asks a teacher a question to which he or she doesn't know the answer!

As Sir Ken Robinson puts it in his TED talk, 'How to Escape Education's Death Valley' (2013): 'If you can light the spark of curiosity in a child, they will learn without any further assistance, very often. Children are natural learners. It's a real achievement to put that particular ability out, or to stifle it. Curiosity is the engine of achievement.'

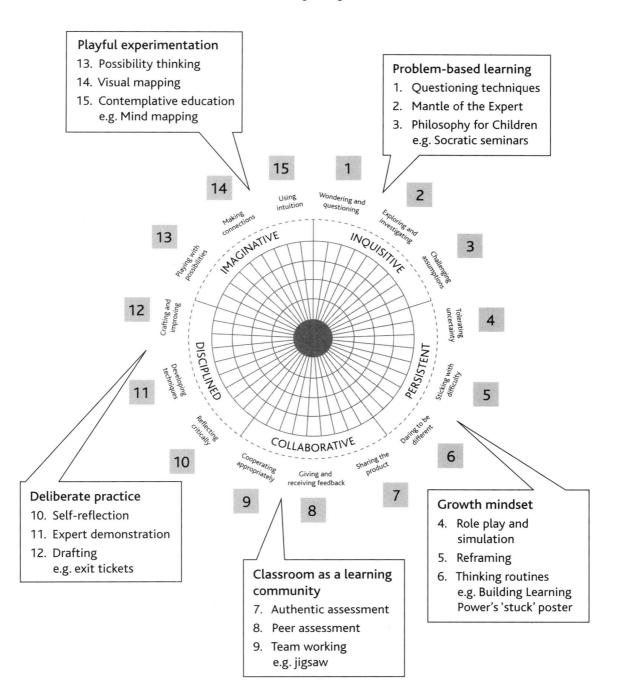

The signature pedagogy: problem-based learning

A core signature pedagogy for creating inquisitive students is problem-based learning. Many of the ideas we have selected for developing inquisitive students are drawn from this approach to teaching.

The core principles of developing inquisitive learners include:

- Relishing problems, challenges and tricky questions to which there are not simple or immediate answers or solutions.

- Valuing questions and questioning at least as much as answers and answering.

- Assuming that knowledge and skills from more than one subject will often be involved and that teachers from two or more subjects may need to collaborate.

- Expecting learners to contribute to the design of sessions, sharing their own questions and their own expertise or interests.

Sub-habit 1: Wondering and questioning

Questioning individuals are not simply curious about things, but pose concrete questions to help them think things through and develop new ideas.

A core approach: questioning techniques

Questioning techniques is a generic term to cover a central aspect of teaching and learning, one that is particularly important to the development of inquisitive learners. Developing confidence in various questioning techniques will be important as you develop students who can wonder and question. As part of this, you may want to be clear about different kinds of questions, of which closed, open, what if, big, wicked and driving are just a few examples.

As well as being core to developing young people who wonder and question, questioning is a teaching strategy with a strong research basis for improving learning outcomes more widely (see Marzano et al., 2001).

Here are five ideas to help you get started.

Starter idea 1: 'I wonder' questions

'I wonder' questions are a simple way of encouraging students to wonder out loud. They are whatever students are wondering about: 'Why are we doing this?' 'How does this link with what we did last week?' 'How does that work?' Before starting any new topic you might like to invite a class to share their 'I wonder' questions verbally or they could be written onto sticky notes and put up on the wall or gathered digitally. These questions will help you to understand what students already know, encourage the habit of wondering and enable the students to make their own connections. Edutopia gives examples from an elementary school in the United States which are helpful.[1]

'I wonder' questions can be further structured by adding in other contextual information, such as the need to formulate questions when you are starting a new topic, when you want to clarify the scope of a question or task, when you are meeting someone new, when you are stuck and so on.

Starter idea 2: Wicked questions

A wicked question or problem is one that does not have an easy answer. It both reflects and stimulates curiosity and might be about meaning and significance. It is a problem worth trying to solve: one that might get under the skin of anyone – teacher, parent or pupil! Questions like these do not have right or wrong answers but instead invite those addressing them to think critically and creatively, exploring different levels of meaning and understanding. Often the same questions are capable of interpretation at different levels by children of different ages – for example: 'Is it OK to bully a bully?' 'What is thinking?' 'Is it good that people are living longer?' 'How else could we group creatures other than as mammals,

---

1   See https://www.edutopia.org/practice/i-wonder-questions-harnessing-power-inquiry.

birds, fish, reptiles and amphibians?' Many of these questions have a philosophical overlay, something we explore in more detail on pages 54–55.

When introducing new learning topics or projects, teachers can begin with a broader philosophical question about knowledge itself: about what we can know and how we can know it. In maths, for example, we can study measurement, but are there some things we cannot measure? In science, are there some things we cannot quantify? If we cannot measure something, do we value it less? In English, what makes a great poem?

Starter idea 3: Driving questions

A driving question is a fundamental question underpinning a project or series of connected activities. This activity aims to get pupils thinking at a macro level about the interrelationships between phenomena under investigation. Let's suppose you were about to embark on an exploratory piece of learning to understand the features of your school's local environment or ecosystem. You might want to pose a question such as, 'What are the different ways that people and plants depend on each other?'

Starter idea 4: Question of the week

Sometimes it's helpful to allow a longer time than a single lesson in which pupils can practise their question asking. Take a moment throughout the day to note good questions. This could be a role for a teacher or student or both. Keep a record of the best questions that are asked in class. Pick one or two and talk about what made it a good question.

Starter idea 5: Cards for questions

At the beginning of the lesson, give out a token or card to each pupil. For each 'good' question that is asked (to the teacher or to the room), the teacher retrieves a card from the pupil who asked it. This helps to engage all pupils in thinking about what they could ask and gives a simple visualisation as to who is asking the questions.

Sub-habit 2: Exploring and investigating

Questioning things alone does not make a creative thinker. Creative individuals act out their curiosity through exploration and follow up on their questions by actively seeking and finding out more.

A core approach: Mantle of the Expert

Mantle of the Expert is a dramatic enquiry-based approach to teaching and learning invented and developed by Professor Dorothy Heathcote at the University of Newcastle in the 1980s. The core idea is that the class do all their curriculum work as if they are an imagined group of experts. In this role, they engage in a task or scenario that gives them opportunities to learn real facts, concepts, skills, responsibilities, language and competencies in a dramatic enquiry-led way. The Mantle of the Expert website gives a number of examples demonstrating that this approach can be adopted in primary and secondary contexts.[2]

This is not to say that school pupils can fully reflect the fundamentally different cognitive processes that real experts go through when solving problems. Of course, there is no short cut to building an expert's huge body of background knowledge. But when pupils assume a role that requires them to think things through differently and engage in new processes, they step up in a way they wouldn't have the opportunity to do so otherwise. It's another way of doing what David Perkins (2009) refers to as 'playing the whole game', and moves learners from theory to experience.

Here are a couple of ideas to help you get started.

---

2   See http://www.mantleoftheexpert.com/about-moe/introduction/what-is-moe-for/.

Starter idea 1: What might you need to know?

As a topic starter, primary children learning about wildlife might be told they will be experts in charge of a small wildlife garden in a local park. You could question them about the kinds of plants and creatures they might need to find out about and suggest a few useful wildlife websites for them to visit.

Starter idea 2: Beginning at the end

A sure-fire way of engaging children is to start with a dramatic end point. This could be a description or a photograph. Simple ideas include a crashed car with just a small girl sitting beside it, a group of people all pointing up into the sky or a group of smartly dressed people, half of whom are laughing and the other half crying. Pupils are then encouraged to adopt an expert persona for the scenario and work back from the evidence they have been given in order to construct a story.

Sub-habit 3: Challenging assumptions

It is important to maintain a degree of appropriate scepticism, not taking things at face value without critical examination.

A core approach: Philosophy for Children

Philosophy for Children (P4C), or some variation of it, is practised in over sixty countries around the world and has a history stretching back over forty years.[3] The underlying principle is for children and young people to experience rational and reasonable dialogue about things that matter to them and their teachers. All participants work together in a 'community of enquiry'. The aim for each child is not to win an argument but to become clearer, more accurate, less self-contradictory and more aware of other arguments and values before reaching a conclusion.

---

3   See https://p4c.com/about-p4c/.

P4C encourages children to create their own philosophical questions which can be examined further, questioned and probed; cannot be answered merely by scientific investigation or sensory data; and relate to the way things are – to issues of reality, meaning, truth, value or knowledge. Over time, teachers notice improved quality and depth of questioning.

Bernadette Russell (2016) recently explored her top ten philosophical questions. We have included five of her favourites here to illustrate P4C approaches:

1. How should we treat animals?
2. What is love?
3. Can kindness change the world?
4. What's the difference between grown-ups and children?
5. Can one person change the world?

Here are two ideas to help you get started.

Starter idea 1: Children create their own philosophical questions

A P4C-type session can be used to introduce any topic or lesson and to consider the concepts within it. In addition, it will help to develop children's thinking, listening, communication skills and ability to consider one question in more depth. Arranging children in a circle means they can see and talk to one another. An artefact, video or audio clip relating to the topic in question can be used as a stimulus. Children discuss their initial reactions to it in pairs to arrive at a question they would like to explore further, which is then recorded for all the group to see. Each pair explains its choice of question and the children vote for the one they would most like to explore further.

The discussion begins by discarding all other questions and asking the pair whose question was chosen to further explain the thinking behind it. The question will provoke class discussion, but if at any point too many are keen to contribute you can direct the children to speak in their pairs before bringing them back into the group.

The discussion can be recorded by a child in the form of a mind map and then summarised by them at the end. The exercise can close by giving children an opportunity to express a final thought.

Starter idea 2: Good or bad

Exploring alternative scenarios enables children to examine critically the things they might take for granted. Even a short exercise like this can challenge some deep-rooted assumptions. Choose a topic that the children are all familiar with, such as modern technology. With a specific piece of technology in mind, and a theme of good or bad, prompt the children to ask their own questions, exploring some of the issues technology brings to bear on our lives.

For younger children, this might be: what would school be like without electricity? Without computers?[4] For older children with access to communication technology: how would life be different without mobile phones? For teenagers? For adults? They might ask: what sorts of things would we have to think about that we don't need to now? What things might we need to be better at if we didn't have instant messaging? In what ways would life be easier/better, and in what ways would life be more difficult/harder? What skills does this technology help or hinder development in? Some children may have limited or no access to this technology and may well have some valuable insights to share!

Persistent

Being persistent is continuing in a course of action in spite of difficulty. Individuals who are tenacious do not give up because of obstacles. Sometimes the barrier to success is a person's own ability, so single-minded resolution to succeed is greatly enhanced by the belief that persistence pays off. An attitude that practice makes

---

[4] You may remember the news story about Silicon Valley parents shunning technology in favour of blackboards and pencils in the classroom. See http://www.nytimes.com/2011/10/23/technology/at-waldorf-school-in-silicon-valley-technology-can-wait.html and https://www.theguardian.com/teacher-network/2015/dec/02/schools-that-ban-tablets-traditional-education-silicon-valley-london.

perfect, stemming from the belief that improvement will come with sufficient effort, is what sets the persistent person apart from someone who gives up when the going gets tough.

Thomas Edison, inventor of the light bulb, had been working on the development of a nickel-iron battery for over five months when an associate visited his lab. With over 9,000 experiments behind him and not one successful result, Edison's reply to an enquiry from his sympathetic associate was: 'Results! Why, man, I have gotten a lot of results! I know several thousand things that won't work' (Dyer and Martin, 1910, p. 615).

Edison was one persistent problem-solver! While we might say that repeated failure built stamina, the quotation above demonstrates how Edison viewed the 'failures' as necessary for learning from and, ultimately, necessary for success.

The signature pedagogy: growth mindset

A core signature pedagogy for creating persistent students relates to the concept of growth mindset (Dweck, 2006; see also Chapter 2). The idea of a growth mindset brings together two strands of what we have called expansive education: seeing intelligence as being learnable and valuing the kinds of capabilities we are calling creative thinking.

Core principles of developing as a persistent learner include:

- Believing in the elasticity of your own intelligence.
- Being willing to make mistakes in order to learn.
- Working at the edge of your comfort zone.
- Using language that reflects the provisional nature of performance: 'I can't *yet*.'

Sub-habit 4: Tolerating uncertainty

Being able to tolerate uncertainty is important when actions or even goals are not fully set out.

Here are three ideas to get you started.

A core approach: role play and simulation

Role play and simulation provide opportunities for students to be exposed to situations in which the instructions are imprecise, where there are no simple or right answers and which require students to act with incomplete information. They also facilitate something important for creative thinking about what might be. By taking the learning 'off-line', role play and simulation allow students to hypothesise and visualise a future situation from a position of safety.

Starter idea 1: Predict future challenges

Uncertainty can be hard to live with, but you can help children by predicting some of the challenges they might come up against and thinking through the actions they might take. A starter activity could focus on something general: transition to secondary school or college, for example. Predictions could include new classes and relationships, new tutors, getting lost on a larger campus or having to fit more study time in alongside other commitments. You can ask pupils to suggest how they might tackle these scenarios.

Starter idea 2: Brainstorming to suspend judgement

While the idea of brainstorming has come in for much criticism for its tendency to promote groupthink and inability to generate sensible ideas, it can be a useful starter activity for learning to suspend judgement and live with uncertainty about *how* something might work. Take a central question or issue and follow whatever threads of thought the pupils lead the discussion along. This could be anything from an alternative history scenario, to a science experiment, to a design for a house, a menu or a design and technology project. Pretend that the ideas might work and see where they take you collectively. Remind pupils that all ideas are potentially good ideas; don't allow evaluative judgements, feedback on ideas or problematising. See if pupils can learn to live with the process and find what is valuable at the end.

Starter idea 3: List as many games as you can

Direct the class to list as many games as they can in two minutes. Respond to any questions with the retort that all instructions have been given and that students should do the best they can with the instructions stated. Upon completion, the students can call out the games and you can write them on the board. Games are likely to fall into several categories, such as board games, computer games, playground games or sports. This exercise tests pupils' ability to deal with ambiguity, where the instructions could be open to a number of different interpretations, and they have to make assumptions. Upon comparing answers, did some pupils find they dismissed certain categories or focused heavily on one in particular? This exercise helps them to see how their own preconceptions, which limit the degree of divergence of their thinking, can also hinder problem-solving and a search for alternatives.

Sub-habit 5: Sticking with difficulty

Persistence in the form of tenacity is important, enabling an individual to get beyond familiar ideas and come up with new ones.

A core approach: reframing

Not everyone has Thomas Edison's seemingly inbuilt lens for seeing failure as an important step on the road to success. Indeed, success in sticking with difficulty requires a mindset shift for many people. To view difficulty as a desirable state of mind – not one that is upsetting or to be avoided – goes against the grain, particularly for those for whom success has tended to come easily, but also for those for whom failure has appeared to be a pattern in life.

Reframing can be explained to learners using the 3 Ps of pervasiveness, personalisation and permanence. Martin Seligman's idea of 'learned optimism' (Seligman, 2006) comes about when you begin explaining your performance like an optimist: 'I'm struggling with this maths question today. I need some more help because I don't think that explanation worked for me,' rather than a pessimist: 'I just don't get maths. Everyone else does. I'm just so terrible at school and I'll never be any good.'

Note that the pessimist uses language that suggests permanence (this sort of thing always happens to me, and it will always be like this), personalisation (things like this always happen to me) and pervasiveness (this happens in everything I do), while the optimist sees the bad situation as temporary, realises the problem is specific and takes only a fair share of the responsibility. Conversely, and this is perhaps where the optimist's mindset is reinforced, a good situation is seen by the optimist as permanent, pervasive and personal.

Starter idea 1: Growth mindset prompts

For learners who are more prone to internalising 'failure' as a permanent characteristic of themselves, the good news is that a growth mindset can be learned. Classroom walls may be decorated with growth mindset posters, and this starter involves handing out growth mindset prompt cards with feedback on pupils' work. It brings the idea to the fore in the minds of learners and is useful whenever the work they are about to undertake is particularly challenging.

Give students feedback on a piece of work they have done recently and hand out cards or sticky notes with prompts to encourage growth mindset thinking. As they read through, ask them to identify any negative thought patterns on the card that they recognise and then reframe their thinking using the questions/prompts on the card. They can then attempt to rework errors, redraft or otherwise continue with their work.

Here are some prompts which you could adapt:

✗ ~~I look stupid for getting this wrong.~~

✓ I am redoing this work to improve my performance, not to look good.

? What's the biggest mistake I've ever made in this lesson? What did I learn from that mistake? How does making mistakes help me learn?

✗ ~~I'm stuck and I don't know what to do next.~~

✓ The best learning happens when I'm challenged.

? What resources have I got access to in order to help myself get unstuck?

✗ ~~I'm never going to get this right.~~

✓ I need to approach this differently.

? How is 'I can't do this yet' different from 'I can't do this'?

✗ ~~I'm not as clever as everyone else.~~

✓ People learn different things at different paces.

? How can I learn from other people's experiences, mistakes and good habits?

✗ ~~I'll never remember all these points.~~

✓ Keep practising and it will become habit!

? How can I practise this more effectively?

✗ ~~I always get this wrong.~~

✓ I'm improving a little bit with every piece of work.

? How can I challenge myself to get this right next time?

Starter idea 2: Expansive questions

One stage on from the prompts we have just been exploring is to draw from a larger bank of questions which you can use to help learners focus on their ability to grow and learn.

- What is working for you?
- Which part are you finding most difficult?
- How might you deal with that aspect?
- Are there any other ways you could approach this sort of difficulty?
- Did you make any mistakes that have helped you learn?
- How could you make this more difficult and stretch yourself a bit more?
- How would you do something like this next time?
- How might this be useful?
- What else can you remember that might help?
- How might you explain your approach to someone else?
- How could I have explained that better to you?
- How do you feel now you've done it?

Sub-habit 6: Daring to be different

Creative thinking demands a certain level of self-confidence as a prerequisite for sensible risk-taking.

A core approach: thinking routines

To develop the confidence to take different views on life, a first step is to understand that all situations present choices. One way of discovering our own comfort and discomfort zones is any kind of classroom debate where students are required to experience perspectives which may not be their own. Thinking routines are one way of building this into habit. Thinking routines don't take up time – they're not activities on their own – although until they are embedded it might seem that way.

All classrooms have their routines – from those that serve to manage behaviour and time management, to those that organise how learning happens. In any classroom there will be many such routines – for example, 'Listen to the teacher then discuss a question with a partner' or 'Read the text then answer the questions.'

While thinking routines are useful in cultivating many of the dimensions of creativity in this book (see the case study examples from Rooty Hill High School and Brunswick East Primary School in Chapter 5), they are especially helpful if you are trying to change a routine – to dare to be different.

Here are three ideas to get you started.

Starter idea 1: What makes you say that?

The thinking routine, 'What makes you say that?' helps students to use evidence-based reasoning and to share their interpretations.[5] The views of others encourage learners to see multiple perspectives. This is typically a whole-class exercise. Ask students to look at a piece of art, an artefact or a poem. This can even work for making scientific observations or examining more conceptual ideas.

The key questions are:

- What's going on? (or, depending on context, what do you see? What do you know?)
- What do you see (or know) that makes you say that?

---

5 For more on this see: http://www.visiblethinkingpz.org/VisibleThinking_html_files/03_ThinkingRoutines/03d_UnderstandingRoutines/WhatMakes/WhatMakes_Routine.html.

This starter is particularly useful for gathering information about how much students know in relation to a new topic.

Starter idea 2: What do you think?

Picture the scene: you have just explained a task to your class, but rather than students immediately starting you are faced with a forest of hands asking you to repeat it or clarify matters. Why? Because this is what they always do! They have not really been listening!

Introduce the idea that you are going to stop answering any of your students' questions (unless it is a matter of life or death!). Instead, you are going to ask them what they think the answer is:

- What's the answer to …? What do you think?
- How can I work out how to …? What do you think?

It's a simple way to build resilience and persistence.

Starter idea 3: Three before me

This variation on 'What do you think?' is the protocol which requires students to try three different approaches to find answers before they ask you to answer something. If you are unsure that they have done this, ask them to tell you what other answers they have already found before you offer one.

Collaborative

Being collaborative is an inherent part of creativity. It is a common misconception that creativity is the territory of the lone wolf, when in reality no idea is created in a vacuum. Whether we take and develop our ideas from those around us or from further afield in space, or indeed time, the creative thinking classroom is one that encourages interactions which spark thinking.

The signature pedagogy: classroom as a learning community

A core signature pedagogy for creating collaborative habits in learners is the development of a classroom learning community. Many of the ideas we have selected for developing inquisitive students are drawn from this approach to teaching.

Core principles of developing collaborative learners through becoming a learning community have been well articulated by Chris Watkins.[6] They include:

- Expecting learners to listen as well as talk.
- Making it safe for people to offer ideas.
- Making collaboration a frequent activity.
- Requiring interdependence among learners for success.
- Having real accountability among peers.
- Making 'explicit a view of learning which is active, strategic, reflective and involving metacognition'.
- Emphasising enquiry 'as a means of learning and coming to know'.

---

6 See http://chriswatkins.net/wp-content/uploads/2015/07/33-Classrooms-as-Learning-Communities.pdf.

This approach is more than simply creating a classroom context in which group work is valued. It genuinely seeks, within the bounds of school structures, to provide more powerful roles for learners as contributors and shapers of school experiences.

Sub-habit 7: Sharing the product

Creative outputs matter, whether they are ideas or things creating impact beyond their creator.

A core approach: authentic assessment

Authentic assessment is an approach to assessment that measures students' capabilities, knowledge or skills in meaningful, real-world contexts. Authentic assessment gives students the chance to experience external expert opinions (as well as their teacher's) and to use a range of methods which may not be of the standard classroom test variety. Typically methods include:

- Presentations
- Interviews
- An article in a newsletter
- A podcast or broadcast
- Displays of work
- Role play
- Presenting a portfolio of evidence

It's likely that you have already incorporated authentic real-world tasks into your classroom, but in most school systems the default approach is often to go for paper-and-pencil or multiple-choice tests rather than more realistic alternatives.

Here are a couple of ideas to get you started.

Starter idea 1: Bringing in an expert

All schools have experts on hand in the form of parents, past pupils, local employers or crafts/sports people, whose roles will qualify them as experts in a whole range of fields. When you are next thinking about an end-of-module or half-term assessment, consider who your experts might be. Reflect on which of the authentic assessment methods might be most appropriate for your children to use.

Bringing in a parent or other expert may not be a quick starter, but it can be a good way to introduce an approach to more authentic learning. In some cases it may be possible to invite experts to bring in examples of their own work.

Starter idea 2: Creating a rubric

Experts use their expertise to provide specialist feedback or assessment. They know what they think of as 'outstanding', 'excellent' or 'sloppy', but they may not have clearly articulated this.

In any kind of assessment, understanding the criteria by which something is being measured is important. The same is true for authentic assessment, although the 'mark schemes' may be different than for, say, a classroom test. The written means by which performance is measured is called a rubric – a scoring scale used to measure performance according to a task-specific set of criteria. The criteria focus on what is being sought.

In history this might be, for example, the number of sources used and their degree of historical accuracy. If you were judging a student giving a presentation to a local history group after a piece of local investigation, then you might want to add in the appropriateness of the communication media used, as well as the confidence with which the presentation was delivered. Then you would need to introduce some simple levels and describe what you are looking for.

Given our focus on being authentic, it may be most fruitful to try out this whole process with a friendly parent or two and work out the rubric as you go along, inviting the students to develop this on the basis of the different 'assessments' they experience.

Sub-habit 8: Giving and receiving feedback

Creative thinkers want to contribute to the ideas of others and to hear how their own ideas might be improved.

A core approach: peer assessment

A surprising proportion of the feedback students receive comes informally from peers. The quality of feedback is naturally variable. It can be helpful and to the point, or not. It is unlikely to relate to their strengths and weaknesses in learning unless they have been specifically taught how to do this.

More formally, of course, peer assessment is the process where students grade and/or mark work – finished or in progress – done by fellow students and give them oral feedback. It is about much more than getting a friend to tick your answers. If taught well it has positive outcomes (Sebba et al., 2008) and works to the benefit of both pupils, as it improves their understanding of course materials and mark schemes as well as their metacognitive, communication and even group-working skills.

As a key element of Assessment for Learning (AfL), peer assessment skills need to be developed if this idea is to help children engage with, and reflect upon, one another's work and learning. Children will need to know exactly what they are looking for before they can identify it and, over time, this process will help them to plan their own work and meet their own targets.

Critique needs to be:

- Kind, helpful and specific.

- Hard on content but soft on the individual.
- Something that all students have a chance at.

Here are four ideas to get you started.

Starter idea 1: Critique work anonymously

Teaching your pupils to peer assess is less threatening if they begin by using some anonymous work from another class or prior year's class. Until they realise the constructive nature of this task, pupils are more likely to be forthcoming if they aren't anxious about offending someone present. Keep a tight focus on a narrow number of criteria. Don't just show them your marking criteria; question them about what a good answer to the question might look like. Help them to think about what an effective evaluation, descriptive paragraph and so on might look like and why. You might like to rein in comments by using an 'off-topic list' that the class could help you to generate. This might include such things as spelling and punctuation or anything that is over and above what the pupil would be expected to produce.

Starter idea 2: Co-create a visual reference of helpful phrases

Start with one or two phrases that pupils can expand upon. Use the collective stock of helpful phrases as a visual display that they can refer to over time (see Dunn, n.d.):

- I like this part, but have you thought of/how does this relate to ...?
- What made you use this word/phrase/connective/simile/metaphor and not another one?
- The best part is when you ...
- I think that next time you ought to think about ...
- I think you've achieved these two success criteria, but I'm not sure about the third. What do you think?

Starter idea 3: Feedforward

Feedforward is an effective way of solving recurring problems collaboratively in groups of four or so. It encourages individuals to focus actively on an issue they are wrestling with and to put it into words. It suggests a form of words, 'You might like to …' which enables good dialogue and keeps comments polite.

Each member of a small group takes it in turn to identify and describe a problem or issue currently being faced in his or her learning. The other members of the group act as advisers offering advice. All advice is accepted by the issue-owner without comment. After three or four minutes, the session stops and the person seeking help reflects on the suggestions he or she has received.

The conversation goes like this: 'My issue/problem is …' (just a sentence). This is followed by several rounds of, 'You might like to …' (helpful suggestions using the all-important word 'might'), after each one of which the issue-owner says, 'Thank you.' Finally, the issue-owner responds along the lines of, 'Thanks very much. I really like the suggestion that I might …'

Starter idea 4: Guided gallery critique

Gallery critique is a simple process whereby students share their work-in-progress with other students in a gallery or part of a classroom or corridor, and their peers are invited to give them feedback, typically in the form of sticky notes with comments. It is an idea suggested by Ron Berger (2003). It works with any discipline, including drafts of writing, artwork, things being made in design and technology, prototypes and so on. Gallery critique is done on the work itself. Drafts are laid out on tables or display boards and students can focus on their peers' work in any order they like.

Before you try it out, it is worth spending some time on the kinds of approaches we have been describing in this section on collaboration. It is important that students appreciate the need to phrase feedback in such a way that they would be prepared to receive it themselves. This is not simply for the sake of politeness – it's no good giving feedback the recipient can do nothing about! When you introduce the idea, you might like to spend some time focusing on the work of a smaller number of students who are happy to share their ongoing work and receive helpful feedback. In this way, as the teacher, you can take the opportunity to help students realise that the tone of feedback really matters.

Before you set up a gallery critique session it is useful if you can show examples of high quality work to stimulate the students to aim high. Sticky notes of different sizes and colours will be helpful. You might like to offer students structures such as:

- I like this because …
- Even better if …
- Have you seen …?

All students sign their feedback to enable follow-up conversations and encourage responsible dialogue. Or you could give students coloured dots to stick on the piece of work they find particularly inspiring, inviting them to share their reflections afterwards.

Follow-up conversations can include questions like:

- What did you find most tricky?
- Is there an aspect you're less happy with, and why?
- What bit are you most satisfied with?
- How might you aim for excellence with this?
- What have you modelled it on?

Sub-habit 9: Cooperating appropriately

The creative individual cooperates with others, taking into account the nature of the group, the kind of problem and the stage the group has reached.

A core approach: team working

Teams in schools tend to mean sports teams, although in many subjects, and as part of co-curricular activity, teams may be required. For some children the business of being selected for a team can be traumatic. A name appears (or does not) on a school team sheet on a noticeboard. Or worse still, two team captains are chosen (normally the biggest, fastest or smartest) and they proceed to choose their team members from a dwindling stock of options. If you are the last to be picked it can be deeply demoralising.

Yet once out of school and in the workplace, it is commonplace for individuals to find themselves in one or more teams working with others on an assignment. A whole series of processes is put in place, often managed by regular team meetings. It soon becomes clear that team working requires a sense of common purpose, a timescale, an agreed set of working processes and, importantly, different roles for different people.

A well-known approach to understanding the different functions required is Belbin Team Roles.[7] The nine team roles are considered important for a successful team, although a person may cover multiple roles. These are:

1. Resource Investigator: Uses inquisitive nature to search for and bring ideas to the team.

2. Teamworker: Brings the team together; spots where input is needed and provides it.

3. Coordinator: Focuses on objectives and effective delegation.

4. Plant: Solves problems creatively.[8]

5. Monitor Evaluator: Takes an objective stance regarding options and decisions.

6. Specialist: Provides in-depth knowledge of an important aspect of the team's work.

---

7 See http://www.belbin.com/about/belbin-team-roles.
8 'Plant' is a strange term used by Belbin to mean a creative problem-solver!

7. Shaper: Brings momentum to the team.

8. Implementer: Strategises ideas into actions in organised timeframes.

9. Completer Finisher: Scrutinises work to give it a cohesive quality.

Here are four ideas to get you started.

Starter idea 1: Six Thinking Hats

This starter uses Edward de Bono's concept of Six Thinking Hats, an approach widely used in schools.[9] The method is effective at getting students to ask questions from a range of perspectives and to understand that, in any group task, there are different roles that can be played.

While the thought process that prompts questioning is clearly one aspect of creative thinking, the thinking hats concept encourages multiple aspects of creative thinking. It is essentially three pairs of hats: facts versus feelings, plusses versus minuses, divergent versus convergent.

This starter can be done as a series of activities or all at once. Choose a problem that teams in your class are working on and assign them different coloured hats from the list below. Use a one word description of each coloured hat that will help the children to keep its purpose in mind. For example:

- Facts: White hat calls for information that is known and needed: like our creative thinking habit 'exploring and investigating', this hat seeks the facts.

- Feelings: Red hat represents feelings, hunches and intuition: seeks to express emotions, fears and dislikes.

- Positive: Yellow hat explores the positives: seeks values and benefits.

- Caution: Black hat makes judgements: seeks potential pitfalls.

---

9 See http://www.debonogroup.com/six_thinking_hats.php.

- Create: Green hat focuses on new ideas: like our creative thinking sub-habit 'playing with possibilities', this hat seeks possibilities and alternatives.

- Understanding: Blue hat focuses on overseeing: seeks to keep control over the collaborative thinking process.

There are multiple ways to use the Six Thinking Hats. For younger children, you could consider incorporating a display with very large, visual representations of the hats – perhaps ones they can interact with, hold, wear or stand on. You might tackle a subject area or problem relevant to your class by naming the problem, holding one particular hat and asking questions of the sort appropriate only to that hat. You could reverse this and ask pupils to identify the hat relevant to your question. When they have understood the concept, reinforce it by requiring them to ask the questions.

To practise the Six Thinking Hats, divide the children into teams of six – or fewer if necessary – and give the class a topical problem to discuss where a solution is required. Let each child pick for themselves a thinking hat (out of a hat) at random. Groups then discuss the problem using questions and statements framed by team members' own category of hat. Advise that the solution reached should naturally follow from the line of discussion. At the end of a given time (which can be kept short for a starter), compare the sorts of questions asked and the solutions reached.

For older students, ensure that half of the groups have all six of the thinking hats, while others have a skewed distribution of hats. For example, you could ensure that one group has two red hat people (feelings/intuition) but no white (facts). At the end of the exercise it would be extremely valuable to spend time asking the groups to discuss, review and feed back on how the imbalance affected their interactions and their final solution (if indeed they arrived at one!).

Starter idea 2: Subject-related thinking hats

Consider where thinking hats could enrich pupils' thinking in your particular subject area. This might be through specific problems that groups of pupils tackle or the bigger questions. For example:

- Geography: Should borders be open or closed to immigration?

- RE: Should there be limits to freedom of speech?
- Biology: How do we determine when life begins?

Starter idea 3: Team-building exercise

Before beginning an extended piece of collaborative work, develop a cooperative climate in the classroom through exercises that build or strengthen acquaintance among students – for example, a challenge to make the tallest tower out of spaghetti or paper straws, or a bridge out of balsa wood and glue that must span a fixed distance across two table tops and support the most weight. Even when students are very familiar with one another they may not necessarily have worked closely together. Engage them in a fun team-building activity where they must achieve non-academic goals or academic ones that are easily achieved.

Starter idea 4: Playing with Belbin

Take Belbin's nine team roles and come up with a word to describe each one that is suitable for the age group you teach. If your children are younger you might prefer to choose animals associated with the different roles. Spend some time on each role, inviting pupils to put its characteristics into language they understand. See if they can think of class members who are particularly good at each role and reflect on what it is the person does when they are in role. See if they can think of famous people with the characteristics of each role.

Select a suitable problem for your class to investigate in groups, something that they can easily accomplish within a lesson. Depending on the size of each group, ask them to choose one of the Belbin roles and play that. Once they have finished the activity, ask them to review the ways in which each role contributed. Ask them whether any of the roles were particularly helpful and whether any were obviously missing.

Disciplined

Being disciplined is about reflecting critically, developing techniques, crafting and improving. Each of these actions can be the focus of a lesson starter. While creative thinking might sound fanciful, the role of divergent thinking is but one part. The ability to practise convergent thinking – to rein in the generation of new and disparate ideas and to begin to link thoughts together to form patterns and rule out dead ends – is a key part of thinking creatively.

An interesting scene in the film *Apollo 13* gives a real-world example of the constraints on creative thinking in this conversation between Mattingley (cut from the original crew but brought in to help with the mission in a capsule simulator) and Young (the chief engineer):

> Mattingley: Have you started on a procedure?
>
> Young: The engineers have tried but it's your ship. We gotta get you in there.
>
> Mattingley: OK, I need the same cold and dark, gimme the exact same conditions they've got in there now and I need present status of every instrument. I need a flashlight. [*Young hands him a large yellow torch.*] That's not what they have up there. Don't give me anything they don't have on board.
>
> Young: Let's get this show on the road, put him in space fellas.
>
> (Quoted in Llinares, 2011, p. 168)

The signature pedagogy: deliberate practice

A core signature pedagogy for creating disciplined students is deliberate practice, and many of our ideas in this section are drawn from this approach to teaching. Deliberate practice goes beyond mere repetition. It is a thoughtful regime of activities designed with the end goal of improving performance. Deliberate practice targets the difficult parts, provides an optimum level of challenge and also gives feedback to the learner about when things are going right, or indeed wrong (Marzano, 2011).

Practice with a purpose extracts the most learning from an experience. So, instead of working through a series of maths questions for half an hour, we're thinking about picking questions that challenge us, choosing the questions that give us exposure to the tricky bits, redoing questions we got wrong before, redoing difficult questions we got right and seeing if we can still do them. Perhaps we are learning a practical skill like knitting. We try with different yarn and needles to make sure our skill is reliable. On a practice piece we might ignore a mistake and try to carry on if we are focusing on making stitches, or we might take the opportunity to see if we can learn to fix the mistake. We can think in reverse or use a book, an online tutorial or a teacher to help us work out what we've done wrong and fix it. We might then deliberately drop or twist a stitch to give ourselves practice at fixing it.

In *Bodies of Knowledge* (2010), Bill Lucas and his colleagues Guy Claxton and Rob Webster identify five different stages of practice:

1. Getting the feel. It is only when you try something out that you begin to develop a mental 'template' of what the action should feel like. This is where watching others can really help your brain to develop that template more easily, so that when you perform the action correctly it just seems to 'click'.

2. Automating. With enough time, determination and repetition the action becomes controlled by subconscious thought to the point where you can simultaneously perform another action at the same time – like driving while having a conversation. The contrast between conscious competence and automated, unconscious competence is seen if you are touch-typing but have never taught yourself where the number keys are!

3. Picking out the hard parts. This is where you unpick what went wrong and work on that part in isolation.

4. Improvising. This is where you vary your routine, the materials you use and playfully experiment to see how things work differently.

5. Doing it for real. This is the part where you put your skills into action. In school this might involve a performance or presentation of what you have learned.

The core principles of developing disciplined learners include:

- Breaking a complex task down into its component parts.

- Targeting the hard parts.
- Practising something in different places.
- Testing.
- Pre-testing (asking questions about something before you work at it to establish preparedness and make the mind more receptive).
- Asking for feedback.

Sub-habit 10: Reflecting critically

Evaluation is the way in which progress can be seen and understood, and the quality of new ideas or novel thinking can be checked. Thinking in a reflective way helps learners to process what they have experienced – to turn it into learning they can identify, to modify their understanding of the world based on what they have experienced or discovered and ideally to transfer their learning beyond the immediate situation.

A core approach: self-reflection

Self-awareness is a valuable skill for children to develop because it helps them to think about what is and is not working, and to find new ways to solve problems. While the hard graft of drafting and rework (which we explore in Sub-habit 12) is one way of developing discipline in the creative thinker, it is equally important to be reflective. Not to *do*, but to take stock and think, 'What if I'd done it this way?' and 'How is this working and not working?'

Here are three ideas to get you started.

Starter idea 1: Learning logs

Student logs or journals are a tool for encouraging reflection. Some students love them, others find them challenging (as do some adults!). To encourage students of any age to keep a learning log, start simple and structured. Encourage them to write three sentences at the end of a lesson, day or unit.

- Something I did really well was …
- Something I could have done better at was …
- Something which surprised me was …

You could model your interest in this by keeping your own log and sharing yours and theirs from time to time.

Starter idea 2: Teacher prompts

The nature of reflection means that it tends to happen during or after a learning event. But as a starter, it can provide a useful moment of pause that engages students in thinking more deeply about what they are about to learn. This may be particularly useful in a lesson split over more than one session, where critical reflection brings pupils back into focus.

First, identify a specific problem or experience relevant to the lesson. This could be an experiment you conducted with students in the previous lesson which you now want them to write up using scientific language. It could be that they are about to conduct a new experiment but you want them to consider some problems they had using equipment or method in previous lessons, and how they could crystallise their earlier experiences into learning. As you self-talk the sorts of problems you might encounter, model your own questioning and reasoning to the students. Be explicit about how you explain your experience to yourself.

Starter idea 3: Scaffolding

We help students to reflect when we show them how to link their current experience and learning to previous learning. This is called scaffolding. Try signalling to learners that they are moving into a reflective phase of learning through visual or auditory cues; some teachers use music or have a period of silent thinking.

Take time to look back to the previous lesson and invite the students to compare outcomes with intended outcomes, to evaluate their use of creative thinking and to think about how what they've done can apply to other situations. In science, don't just look at equipment and method in a failed experiment. Conduct a discussion about how (whether!) they monitored their own problem-solving and how they focused on getting better at learning.

Sub-habit 11: Developing techniques

Creative thinkers practise a range of conceptual and practical skills in order to improve. Classrooms which seek to encourage this tend to be set out more like a workshop than a typical class (see our ten-dimensional framework on page 8), although there are no hard and fast rules. It is common to see work-in-progress so that it is possible for pupils to understand the progression from novice to expert. This may mean having secure spaces where physical artefacts can be on display or, if it is more theoretical, this could involve displays or video recordings of the skill in action.

A core approach: expert demonstration

'Learning by imitation is regarded as the cornerstone of human cognition' (Tidemann and Ozturk, 2008, p. 380). Not just in infancy, but throughout our lifetimes, watching others is a significant part of learning. Imitation – putting into practice what we see – involves observing, thinking, imagining, remembering and practising. Watching an expert can be helpful, but experts sometimes have their limitations. They may struggle to slow down what they are doing or put themselves in the shoes of the learner. They are 'unable to show the mistake, only the right way' (Sennett, 2008, p. 181).

Expert demonstration is most helpful when accompanied by insightful commentary that helps learners to see where mistakes might occur, what common errors are and how to spot them and how not to do things, as well as what success looks like. Lois Hetland and colleagues (2007) have shown how expert demonstrations – referred to as 'demonstration-lectures' – are an essential part of studio teaching (along with practical making and group critique).

Here are two ideas to get you started.

Starter idea 1: Copying

There are many ways to hone the skills of observation and accurate copying. Activities that give pupils an opportunity to be the 'expert' can – if the purpose is explained to them – help them to appreciate the difficulty of communicating what they are doing to those in the 'learner' role, and perhaps to recognise these when back in the shoes of the learner. For example:

- Copying colour patterns: Younger pupils can practise their observation skills by translating a coloured pattern on a grid onto a blank grid. These can be made more complex using lines instead of coloured blocks or shapes that don't sit neatly on the grid.

- Copying incomplete patterns: Partial patterns can be completed using rules of symmetry.

- Dance: While dance is not exclusively about copying (indeed, there are debates about the extent to which dance training should emphasise creative and choreographic skills over the current emphasis on performance and technique (Watson et al., 2012)), much beginner dance training is a discipline in copying.

Starter idea 2: Slow writing

Slow writing encourages students to think about their technique, and with a little imagination it can be adapted for a range of subject areas, not just writing for

English language which was the context for its development.[10] It encourages them to think about *how* to write, not just *what* to communicate.

Writing is double spaced so the students can come back to each sentence and interrogate every word, phrase or idea to see if a better choice might be found. Ask them to write a number of sentences, each meeting one criterion on a list. In an English language context, criteria might include the number of words, the tense, the punctuation or other grammatical form required on a given topic. In a history context, this might include an evaluative sentence, a sentence that offers a comparison with another time period and so on.

Sub-habit 12: Crafting and improving

Craftspeople take pride in their work, attend to details, practise thoughtfully, are happy to make several drafts or prototypes of their work and work hard to correct any errors.

Crafting and improving is also about valuing excellence. In *An Ethic of Excellence*, Ron Berger says:

> I believe that the work of excellence is transformational. Once a student sees that he or she is capable of excellence, that student is never quite the same. There is a new self-image, a new notion of possibility. There is an appetite for excellence. After students have had a taste of excellence, they're never quite satisfied with less; they're always hungry. (2003, p. 8)

When learners experience success like this — and the intrinsic reward it brings — willingness to put in more hard work and further success are the outcomes we hope to see.

---

10 This term was coined by David Didau (2012).

A core approach: drafting

We mentioned the case of Austin's Butterfly in Chapter 1, a well-known YouTube phenomenon brought to us by educator Ron Berger. But as well as demonstrating the importance of group critique for improvement, the vehicle through which this improvement happens is repeated drafting. Redrafting involves a willingness to recover from failure or criticism at each new draft. It's easy to see repeated drafts as a waste of time; we think we can short cut the learning process if we just show learners what they've done wrong or could have done better, and hope they will bear it in mind next time. But, in reality, the learning is only cemented by arriving at that final 'perfect' piece. Furthermore, learners who are quick to quit tend to learn more slowly and less deeply than those who are willing to engage in the process of trying again and again.

Here are two ideas to get you started.

Starter idea 1: Breaking it up

A focus on deliberate practice could be incorporated into a starter as you think about a task you're going to ask pupils to do. Get them to think about breaking it down – what they might find difficult and how they might practise those parts. Alternatively, you could ask them to do the same exercise for a skill they are trying to develop outside of the classroom, be it goal-keeping in football, practising a difficult piece on an instrument, learning lines for a play, knitting a scarf and so on.

Starter idea 2: Reworking

A simple but overlooked starter activity – typically because of time constraints – is the returning of students' work for redrafting/reworking. Despite these pressures, student time spent addressing your feedback (or their peers' or whoever has marked their work) is some of the most valuable time they will spend. Maybe rework problems from last week! For example, a student support specialist in maths at Rochester Institute of Technology writes, 'You had mastered these problems, remember? Can you still do them without any help?' (Pennington,

2016). This is exactly the sort of work that can justifiably be set for homework if it runs beyond the time in a starter.

Imaginative

Imaginative is perhaps the easiest dimension of creative thinking to remember; creativity involves using your imagination to fuel the journey from inspiration to idea.

As Einstein famously said: 'Imagination is more important than knowledge. For knowledge is limited, whereas imagination embraces the entire world, stimulating progress, giving birth to evolution. It is, strictly speaking, a real factor in scientific research' (2009 [1931], p. 97).

The signature pedagogy: playful experimentation

A core signature pedagogy for developing imaginative students is playful experimentation. The phrase 'playful experimentation' is one that we have coined to describe an approach to learning which has experimentation and a willingness to look for connections as key. Another synonym for this idea might be tinkering. As well as requiring our conscious attention, playful experimentation assumes that we also learn intuitively or non-consciously.

Core principles of developing imaginative learners include:

- Valuing the thought involved in testing and play as much as the final product.
- Allowing time off-task for thoughts to evolve.
- Giving learners the opportunity to select their own tools and equipment.
- Valuing alternative approaches.

Sub-habit 13: Playing with possibilities

Coming up with novel ideas involves putting thoughts together in unusual and interesting ways.

A core approach: possibility thinking

The concept of possibility thinking – or 'what if' and 'as if' thinking – generates novelty and is at the core of creativity in education. Anna Craft and her colleagues (2013, p. 538) describe possibility thinking as 'driving creativity in the classroom'. It's about generating creative thinking by stopping to ask 'What if …?' in order to shift from what *is* to what *might be*.

Teaching possibility thinking involves creating 'an inclusive learning environment' in which:

- Children's experiences and ideas are highly valued.
- Dialogue between children and between children and teachers is encouraged.
- An ethos of respect is nurtured and children as well as teachers experience meaningful control, ownership, relevance and innovation in learning. (Craft and Chappell, 2016, p. 409)

Teachers create certain boundaries within which there are options to explore – be it with scientific equipment, baking ingredients or numbers.

Here are two examples to get you started.

Starter idea 1: Classic paper clip game

Thinking of alternative uses for a simple item such as a paper clip is one of the most famous indicators of one aspect of creativity – divergent thinking. Give each pupil a paper clip and ask them to jot down as many uses for it as they can, other than clipping paper together. Depending on the age and mood of your class you may need to give them a few examples to get them going. It could be a guitar pick, a SIM card eject tool, a headphone cable-tidy, a key ring, a marker for the end of a roll of sticky tape and so on. Give them two minutes before asking them to share all their ideas. Other commonly used alternatives to a paper clip include objects such as a chair, a mug or a brick.

Starter idea 2: '5 Whys' technique

Developed by Toyota founder Sakichi Toyoda in the 1930s, the '5 Whys' technique aims to build in-depth understanding of the processes and conditions on the shop floor, rather than reflecting what someone in a boardroom thinks might be happening. It is remarkably simple: when a problem occurs, you uncover its nature and source by asking 'why' no fewer than five times. By sticking to this simple line of questioning you encourage imaginative root cause analysis.

A pupil-related example to get you going might look like this. A pupil arrives late for a lesson:

1. Why? Because I missed the bus.
2. Why? Because I had an argument with my mum.
3. Why? Because I had not got my school bag ready and she wanted to leave the house.
4. Why? Because I went to bed too late.
5. Why? Because I was playing on my Xbox.

The pupil is then in a position to fix the root cause. You can try the '5 Whys' on similar simple issues or you can use it on complex issues such as:

- Why is the planet getting hotter?
- Why are there so many migrants without homes?
- Why do people sleep on the streets?

Sub-habit 14: Making connections

Seeing new links between ideas is an important aspect of the synthesising process of creative thinking.

A core approach: visual mapping

An important capability is that of drawing together ideas to make a new idea or a new product. This might be assembling notes to make an orderly file from which to study, arranging the logical flow of ideas for an essay, or choosing which element of a problem should be tackled first and the information and steps needed to solve it. Often it is helpful to be able to represent ideas or concepts visually. For example, an essay plan may be represented using a series of sticky notes with key words signifying arguments and significant theories. A book plan might include chapter headings, short summaries and key concepts. The writer can then organise ideas into a logical flow.

Making connections requires us to hold two or more ideas in our head at the same time and see how they relate to each other. It's also about using ideas to make plans. Planning is the backbone of much of what happens in the real world – from architectural concept into a construction project, a course syllabus translated into a scheme of work or a book concept contracted by a publisher to a book plan. But in life we are rarely presented with a full set of ingredients and a method to follow; the many unknowns of the real world mean that creative thought is key to bringing ideas together in ways that are helpful and sometimes novel. This is where the ability to make links between seemingly disparate elements is needed. And for many people being able to see ideas visually is useful.

Here are four ideas to get you started.

Starter idea 1: Sequencing an assignment

Some pupils will feel more at ease with their workload if they can see a visual representation of the sequence of activities in an assignment or series of assignments in a course. Help them to break down a piece of work into a bar chart which they can fill in as they complete the various stages required. For older students, a Gantt chart is a way of representing work completed in certain periods of time, taking into account tasks that must happen before others. This will help them to make connections in their mind between pieces of work.

Starter idea 2: Odd one out

This activity can be adapted but it essentially involves students having to make connections between objects or concepts in order to decide which does not belong.

For younger children, you could choose three objects with a common theme – categories such as animals, paintings, buildings, trees, monarchs or vehicles perhaps. The choice is endless, and it works well if it relates to a topic you are studying – for example, in design and technology, food that comes from plants versus food that comes from animals. It's helpful if you have in mind why one of the three might be different from its neighbours but are also ready to listen out for alternative ideas. The pertinent point is that children are able to express their rationale for selecting the odd one out.

Starter idea 3: Connections

Using similar thought processes to 'Odd one out', this activity involves students having to construct connections between objects or concepts. These can be seemingly, as well as actually, unconnected, increasing the concentration required to 'find' a relationship which may have to be cleverly constructed!

For example, for each of the lists below, what fourth word is related to each of the previous three?[11]

1	House	Village	Golf	?
2	Key	Wall	Precious	?
3	Dance	Snow	Base	?
4	End	Burning	Cook	?
5	Birthday	Hunting	Line	?
6	Call	Line	Pay	?
7	High	Man	Wheel	?

For older students, pair them up or assign small groups and introduce a team challenge. You could award winners based on speed, which would emphasise quick and intuitive thinking. Alternatively, you might allow a vote (with you holding the casting vote if necessary) for the group showing the most originality.

The aim is to be the first group to make creative connections between ten objects chosen at random. These might be physical objects in the classroom, pictures of objects or ones you pick out of a hat. To increase the challenge of connection-making, you could name concepts rather than objects.

Starter idea 4: What does this remind you of?

This comprehension exercise will help students to make connections between a text, themselves, other texts and the wider world, deepening their understanding of the material. Take a piece of text related to your subject area and ask the students to think about the following questions. These can be adapted depending on the genre of the text which does not need to be limited to fiction. You can also begin by modelling each type of connection, focusing particularly on the difference

---

11 Answers: 1. Green, 2. Stone, 3. Ball, 4. Book, 5. Party, 6. Phone, 7. Chair.

between connections that shed light on the piece ('I can relate to this character because his experience taught him ...') and those that are merely surface level ('I am the same age as the main character').[12]

Relating the text to themselves:

- What does the piece remind you of?
- Do you relate to any of its characters or themes?
- Does the piece relate to anything in your own life on some level?

Relating the text to other texts:

- Does the content of the text, or its characters or themes, remind you of something else you have read?
- How is the writing style similar to other things you have read?
- How is the piece different from other things you have read?

Relating the text to the wider world:

- Does the piece remind you of (other) real-world scenarios/events?
- How is the piece relevant to us today?
- How are the events/characters/themes different from (other) real-world scenarios/events?

This exercise can be used as the basis for essay writing.

Sub-habit 15: Using intuition

The use of intuition allows individuals to make new connections tacitly that would not necessarily materialise using analytical thinking alone. As an adult,

---

12 This exercise is expanded further at http://www.readwritethink.org/professional-development/strategy-guides/making-connections-30659.html, where additional resources can be found.

we somehow know that a new house is right for us before we have done all our rational calculations. As a child, we pick up on a friend's unspoken anxieties without having to describe how we know that they are suppressing a feeling of sadness. Intuition can often be misunderstood as anti-intellectual and lazy. In fact, it is just a different way of making sense of the world, often based on stored knowledge and memories which are nevertheless difficult to access formally. It's easy to undervalue in a classroom setting, as this exchange reminds us:

> Boy looking out of classroom window.
>
> Teacher: What are you doing, boy?
>
> Boy: Thinking, sir.
>
> Teacher: Well, stop it!

A core approach: contemplative education

Recent comprehensive research into the impact of contemplative education (CE) in schools showed that meditation is beneficial in three areas: increased well-being, better social skills and greater academic success (Waters et al., 2015). Meditation in this context means the deliberate act of regulating attention on to internal or external phenomena. Full concentration is involved, as individuals observe thoughts, emotions and body states.

Meditation is a way of slowing down busy minds so that they can operate in a different mode and more readily access intuition. A surprisingly large number of Nobel Prize winners attribute their breakthrough thinking to moments of intuition. Rita Levi-Montalcini, who received the Nobel Prize for Medicine in 1986, is said to have reflected: 'You've been thinking about something without willing to for a long time … Then, all of a sudden, the problem is opened to you in a flash, and you suddenly see the answer' (quoted in Fensham and Marton, 1992).

In classrooms, it is helpful to create more moments when ideas can be incubated and to find ways of slowing down the frantic pace of school life. Indeed, if we hope to nurture intuition in children 'it is essential to make room for exploration and feelings, not only for analysis and memorization' (Cloninger, 2006, p. 26).

Here are three ideas to get you started.

Starter idea 1: Waiting time

Often associated with AfL, the idea of waiting time – which encourages students to reflect silently before answering questions – pre-dates AfL. When inviting pupils to answer questions, yours or theirs, teach them to wait three seconds before answering. For many, three seconds is actually quite a long time not to be able to speak their thoughts out loud and you may need to model and practise it with some kind of timer. It turns out that waiting like this encourages more pupils to answer, improves the quality of answers and, by slowing down the pace, encourages different kinds of creative thinking.

Starter idea 2: Noticing everything

This simple exercise requires something to focus on – this could be an interesting object (a potted plant, a garment, a photograph) or even the sound of the birds outside. Something multisensory that pupils can see, touch, hear or even smell can be more of a stimulus. Ask them to tune out everything else around them and focus on the object. What do they notice? What can they see? Ask them if they can see the dew on the petals, the detail on the lace, the subtle difference in colour, the light falling and making shadows.

This exercise can be done during a routine physical activity – for example, sharpening a pencil, tidying up or eating a piece of fruit. During the activity, the pupils can try asking themselves: what am I doing? What are my hands and my body doing, and why? They might notice themselves slipping out of concentration and back into autopilot. Can they bring themselves back into focusing on the physical sensations?

Starter idea 3: Visualise

This exercise will put pupils in a receptive state to absorb detail. Hand out copies of a descriptive passage in a book. Read the passage out loud, then ask the pupils to read it slowly to themselves. Tell them to close their eyes at the end of each sentence and try to visualise what they have just read. After a given time, ask them to close their eyes again and now picture what happens next …

Some pupils might wish to share where they think the text might go next. Where anything was ambiguous in the description, ask them to offer their own perceptions to the class.

Finish by reading the next section of the book so they can see how the author actually played out the scene. How was it different? Did anybody's intuition lead them correctly? Maybe there were subtle clues or cues in the text – did anybody pick them up?

In this chapter we have explored each of the fifteen sub-habits of creative thinking and made some suggestions as to how schools typically start out. In the next chapter, we look at ways of embedding practices, especially at leadership level and in professional learning.

Chapter 4
Going Deeper

Some more extended examples

> There is no doubt that creativity is the most important human resource of all. Without creativity there would be no progress, and we would be forever repeating the same patterns.
>
> Edward de Bono, *Sur/petition: Going Beyond Competition* (1993, p. 169)

Schools that are committed to developing the capabilities of their pupils will want to embed creative thinking more systematically in all of their teaching and create opportunities for it in both the curriculum and co-curriculum. Once there is a good enough familiarity with the kinds of approaches we discussed in the last chapter, staff tend to want to go deeper with their practices.

In this chapter, we focus on a few of the different ways in which schools choose to go deeper with these ideas. Within the school, this might involve looking at different aspects of practice across the spectrum of areas such as professional development and leadership. We now take a look at how creativity might become a focus in each of these areas:

- Leadership for creative thinking.
- Professional development for creative thinking.
- Exploring signature pedagogies for cultivating creative thinking.
- Engaging parents with the idea of creative thinking.
- Co-curricular experiences for creative thinking.

Leadership for creative thinking

Leadership permeates everything in schools. While teachers themselves can have a great impact in, for example, engaging parents or exploring signature pedagogies for creative thinking in the classroom, support and direction from the leadership team can ensure the whole school is moving in the right direction.

Trying out signature pedagogies in the classroom requires teachers who are willing, capable and encouraged to give it a go. School leadership steers professional development through its investment in staff professional learning, through its direction and focus for that professional learning and by facilitating time for collaborative planning. The decisions that leaders make will impact professional development and opportunities for reflection and collaboration through professional learning communities.

Leaders also set the tone through the language they use (e.g. is it indicative of a growth mindset?), the setting of vision and values and potentially some policy decisions. They have a major role to play in determining the culture that parents experience and become part of (or don't engage with) during their time at the school, as well as the attitudes pupils adopt towards their learning and themselves as learners.

Creative leadership and leading for creativity

There are all sorts of barriers to creativity in the classroom. Just as a mandate to develop and embed creativity in the classroom will fall flat without teacher support, so creativity is unlikely to flourish without the support of school leadership.

Louise Stoll and Julie Temperley (2009, p. 64) suggest that school leaders 'need to be able to unlock creativity in their staff in order to enhance learning. And to lead a creative school, you need creative leadership.' Yet there is no objective definition of what it means to be a creative leader. Stoll and Temperley's own evidence suggests a number of ways head teachers can nurture creativity:

- Model creativity and risk-taking. This means, for example, that heads are living out their risk-taking and 'not compromising it'; that they don't 'revert to type' when there's a phone call from Ofsted (ibid., p. 65).[1] During interview, most of Stoll and Temperley's teachers told them that the greatest risk of innovating their practice was that 'we won't cover the curriculum' (ibid., p. 74). Yet many paused on realising what they had said, recognising that this was not such a big risk, it wasn't important and it was easily rectifiable.

- Simulate a sense of urgency – if necessary, generate a crisis. This is where problem-finding is important and problem-solving is a stimulus for creativity.

- Expose colleagues to new thinking and experiences. This could be from other teachers, teachers in other departments/faculties, bringing in ideas from research or swapping ideas with – or bringing in/observing – colleagues in local schools.

- Self-consciously relinquish control. Allow teachers to try new things without feeling that every 'failure' is being watched and noted. Even better, encourage colleagues to share their learning from so-called failure with others.

- Provide time and space and facilitate the practicalities. This might mean deadlines (creativity sometimes benefits from a little pressure), but not targets which promote linear thinking.

- Promote individual and collaborative creative thinking and design. Creativity doesn't happen in a vacuum and colleagues stimulate one another's thinking. But time for personal reflection and idea development is needed as well, as is coming back together to keep ideas focused.

- Set high expectations about the degree of creativity. Innovation must be valued.

---

1 The Office for Standards in Education, Children's Services and Skills, England's school inspection agency.

- Use failure as a learning opportunity. This means valuing things that go wrong and giving individuals an opportunity to put things right.
- Keep referring back to core values. Creative efforts need to have a clear and common direction.

Focusing on a single dimension of creative thinking

Besides nurturing a culture of creativity, leaders can steer the school in more practical and immediate ways. An example might be having a school-wide creative theme over a week or half term, where one of the five dimensions of creative thinking is explored in some way at every opportunity. There might be implications for assemblies, tutor time, lesson debriefs, staff meetings, newsletters to parents and systems of reward.

Professional development for creative thinking

The teacher as a learner

In the introduction we presented a ten-dimensional framework to help teachers reflect on the choices they make regarding learning methods (see page 8). While it is possible to see this as just a series of choices, there is a deeper understanding of professional practice embedded in this framework, one which is embodied in a general move to the left of the figure.

The role of the teacher *as a learner* is a fundamental reframing of teaching from a directive approach that is focused on meeting standards, to a facilitative approach 'in which the full potential of the learner can be realized' (Gale, 2001, p. 106). Donald Schön's (1984) idea of the 'reflective practitioner', using 'reflection-in-action' thinking while doing, is central here, as is David Kolb's (1984) idea of the learning cycle.

Action research, also known as teacher enquiry, is a very practical way for teachers to engage in an ever-improving cycle of action and reflection upon their own professional practice. This approach requires leadership to lead, support and engage with teachers. Without this, teachers find themselves at risk of going against the norm. Gale quotes Schön's thoughts on the teacher who takes a creative approach to professional practice: 'What happens in such an educational bureaucracy when a teacher begins to think and act not as a technical expert but as a reflective practitioner? Her reflection-in-action poses a potential threat to the dynamically conservative system in which she lives' (Gale, 2001, p. 109).

John Hattie reminds us that this reframing of the role of the teacher is not a nice-to-have, but is vital. Reflecting on his drawing together of over 800 meta-analyses of studies relating to achievement, he concludes that 'The remarkable feature of the evidence is that the biggest effects on student learning occur when teachers become learners of their own teaching' (Hattie, 2009, p. 22). So this is not merely about being creative for its own sake, 'but for us to learn from what makes the difference when teachers innovate' (ibid., p. 24).

This is what good teachers are doing all the time:

- Doing something innovative (or new to you) in your teaching practice.
- Looking at what is working and what is not.
- Looking for contrary evidence.
- Making changes as needed.
- Being aware of the effects of your innovation: looking for both intended and unintended consequences.

And to spread the success wider:

- Finding ways to capture feedback.
- Sharing findings with colleagues.

As Hattie puts it: 'those teachers who are students of their own effects are the teachers who are the most influential in raising students' achievement ... the excellent teacher must be vigilant to what is working and what is *not* working in the classroom' (ibid., p. 24).

Personal development and real-world learning

When it comes to being creative about teaching creative thinking, it's also about personal development. Throughout secondary education there is much pressure on young people to develop interests outside of school. Careers guidance counsellors emphasise the importance of having content 'for your CV', and besides exam results – the pinnacle of school achievement (in the UK) – is that all-important 'personal statement' required on the UCAS application form (and, of course, other jurisdictions have the same requirement for this ability to balance academic performance with extra-curricular activities).[2] It's easy to see extra-curricular activities as just a means to an end and to overlook why we call them 'interests'. The idea is that having these interests is what makes us well rounded. The same applies to teachers: research has shown that having hobbies and interests is what makes people innovative in their field of employment (Henriksen and Mishra, 2013).

Danah Henriksen and Punya Mishra (2013) propose five approaches for creative teaching, and these relate strongly to the idea of making connections with real life through your outside interests. With all these ideas, teachers need to think about how teaching creatively can help them teach creative dispositions to pupils.

1. Connect your interests with your teaching. According to Henriksen and Mishra, the research shows that the most accomplished people in a field are also highly creative outside of their profession. Award winners in a National Teacher of the Year competition had a variety of creative interests

---

[2] According to the UK's Universities and Colleges Admissions Service (UCAS), the personal statement is 'a piece of text applicants write to show why they're applying and why they'd be a great student for a course provider to accept'. See https://www.ucas.com/corporate/about-us/who-we-are/ucas-terms-explained.

'which they actively incorporated into classroom lessons and practices'. It's not about using a traditionally 'creative' medium (e.g. art or music) to do something cutting edge, but about making connections between what you are teaching and what your hobbies and interests have taught you. New teachers can be given the freedom to try this out by asking them to plan a lesson that connects a given topic with an outside interest.

2. Link lessons to real-world learning. Consider ways – both large and small – to connect your topics to real-life events. In many cases, topics are open to the gathering of empirical data by observing or measuring the land or people around you.

3. Cultivate a creative mindset. This is about sifting experiences as they happen – making time to consciously reflect on things you read, observe and notice. All sorts of things might serve as a stimulus for (creatively) teaching creativity in class.

4. Value collaboration. Build a creative community where teachers can share ideas – things they've trialled and things they'd like to have a go at. Regular meetings that span faculty borders can open up possibilities for collaboration and new ideas. Many schools have focused professional learning communities, although there is good evidence that this may be more difficult in secondary schools where compartmentalisation along departmental lines is common and there may be a lack of common cause or even trust between departments (Stoll and Temperley, 2009).

5. Take intellectual risks. Just as leaders must do this, so must teachers if they are to develop their creative practice. Furthermore, teachers who take intellectual risks serve as role models to pupils for numerous aspects of creative thinking. For example, how can you play with possibilities, challenge assumptions, tolerate uncertainty, dare to be different or share the product without some degree of risk?

Exploring signature pedagogies for cultivating creative thinking

To recap, the signature pedagogies relating to each of the five dimensions of creativity are:

1. Inquisitive: problem-based learning.

2. Persistent: growth mindset.

3. Collaborative: classroom as a learning community.

4. Disciplined: deliberate practice.

5. Imaginative: playful experimentation.

We now look a little more practically at some ways in which teachers of any subject, working at different stages of education, can launch a scheme of work by giving more step-by-step guidance on some different starter activities. The idea here is that we take one of the five signature pedagogies and make it part of the school's teaching and learning strategy.

A problem-based learning approach: Socratic seminars

Socrates believed in the power of asking questions as a way of acquiring knowledge. Socratic seminars are formal discussions, stimulated by a text, in which the teacher (or student) asks open-ended questions. Students listen closely to the comments of others, thinking critically for themselves, and articulate their own thoughts and their responses to the thoughts of others. The approach works well when it is based on an authentic, ambiguous or perhaps controversial piece of text, which learners might be asked to read and annotate beforehand. After a while the students can be encouraged to run the seminars themselves. The seminar begins with a question, ideally chosen so that it relates to the lives of learners, allowing them to bring in their own experiences of the world. The value of the questions is in the discussion they facilitate, not in any definitive answer they might provide.

It may be helpful to start by offering students a phrase bank on which they can draw to build their confidence and fluency. These might include:

Socratic seminar phrase bank

Checking understanding	So I think you are saying that …
	What I am hearing is …
Supporting others	I like what Amy is suggesting and …
	I see what you mean and …
Building on others	That's a good idea and I …
	I agree with what you are saying and would add that …
Taking a different line	I can understand where you are coming from but …
	That's an unusual idea but I really can't agree …

A growth mindset approach: Building Learning Power's 'stuck' poster

Building Learning Power is the inspiration of Guy Claxton. In a seminal book, Claxton (2002) laid out his idea of what powerful learners do. Rather than the 3 Rs historically associated with academic success, he suggested a different set and added a fourth one: resilience, resourcefulness, reflectiveness and reciprocity. Schools quickly took to these ideas, seeing how they could infuse every subject with these powerful learning dispositions.

At the core of being a resilient learner is being able to keep going when you get stuck, or – as is attributed to Jean Piaget as a definition of intelligence – 'knowing what to do when you don't know what to do'. One school took this idea and worked with its pupils to create a 'stuck' poster to which the children contributed their ideas for getting unstuck. It has become widely imitated.

> What good learners do:
> ✓ Listen to others
> ✓ Ask as well as answer questions
> ✓ Cooperate with others
> ✓ Ask yourself where you went wrong and why
> ✓ Don't give up when you are stuck
>
> You could:
> ✓ Read the question again
> ✓ Split the question into smaller bits
> ✓ Ask someone who has a similar problem
> ✓ Ask yourself: what do I already know that could help me?
> ✓ Go on to another question and come back to the bit you are stuck on at the end

Stuck poster

Source: Claxton (2002, p. 72)

You don't have to copy these ideas exactly. Indeed, it is much better if they can emerge out of discussions with your class. Essentially, you are asking pupils to pool their strategies and, by implication, develop a personal list which works for each individual. You could try it with a class and then put a collective version on the wall or encourage individuals to create their own. These could be on paper, sticky notes or tablets.

A variant of this approach is used on the TV show *Who Wants to Be a Millionaire?* When contestants get stuck they choose one of three options: phoning a friend, going 50-50 or asking the audience. And, of course, like the ideas on the poster, these are all good learning strategies.

A classroom as a learning community approach: jigsaw

In the 1970s, Elliot Aronson and his students at the University of Texas and the University of California devised the jigsaw classroom, a research-based cooperative learning technique. As with a jigsaw puzzle, the part played by each student is crucial for the completion and full understanding of the final product.[3]

The class is divided into a number of 'home groups'. The teacher introduces the topic or problem that will be investigated by the teams, and explains that the problem will be subdivided into smaller elements. Group members choose which sub-topic to research and then reassign themselves with the rest of the class into new working groups by sub-topic. So now there are 'home groups' – put on hold while the research takes place – and 'expert groups' where material is researched and studied, ready for teaching to the rest of each pupil's home group. After knowledge is shared by each home group member – so that each member of the class has a working knowledge of all the sub-topics – all students are tested individually on the full set of material.

The beauty of the jigsaw approach is that it fosters both autonomy and team working. It motivates each individual pupil to investigate his or her own sub-topic in sufficient detail to be able to relay back to their home group. Desire to understand their own individual topic is enhanced because the home group are relying on each member's ability to teach the material in order to succeed in the topic test!

---

3   For more on the jigsaw classroom see: www.jigsaw.org.

A key element required for jigsaw's success is, of course, pupils' competence at teaching their peers. Learners need to be coached in some key skills involved in teaching (as well as learning from their peers), including questioning and giving explanations (Souvignier and Kronenberger, 2007).

The use of questioning routines is helpful here, such as:

1. What does … mean?
2. Explain why …
3. Explain how …
4. How are … and … similar?
5. What is the difference between … and …? (Souvignier and Kronenberger, 2007, p. 761)

These can be introduced in advance of the construction of jigsaw teams. Elmar Souvignier and Julia Kronenberger, who devised the set of five question stems above, suggest an introductory lesson that does the following:

- Establishes the sequence of listening–asking–responding that expert team teaching interactions should follow.

- Explains the five question stems and their purpose.

- Practises the five question stems. For example, use a game where a piece of text is made visible to all pupils, who take it in turns to be allocated a question stem which they must use to pose a question about the text.

During the jigsaw process itself, visual prompts can be used (e.g. laminated cards with the five question prompts for each home group's table).

Souvignier and Kronenberger's research found that even for very young children (third grade), the jigsaw approach was comparable to teacher-guided instruction in terms of test performance. But we know that test results for content knowledge are not the only desirable outcome. Cooperative learning within a team, as well as the ability to present your own knowledge as an 'expert', are of great value in the real world. Used carefully for particular content, the jigsaw approach can be a worthwhile signature pedagogy.

A deliberate practice approach: exit tickets

In order to develop critical reflection – both pupils' and the teacher's – exit tickets (or slips) are useful for prompting thinking about what teachers and pupils need to do next. Exit tickets can be as simple as a small piece of paper or index card on which students respond to a teacher prompt.

Tickets serve a number of purposes depending on the prompt used:

- Prompts to rate students' current understanding of new learning. They provide an easy way for teachers to find out what students have understood from a lesson and how to orient future lessons to address areas of confusion. The teacher forms the prompt, or question, around whatever feedback is likely to be most useful for setting up the next lesson's learning.

- Prompts to analyse and reflect on students' efforts around the learning. They can make end-of-session reflection routine. Prompts aimed at student self-reflection can cover such things as effort levels, metacognitive awareness or learning strategies.

- Prompts to provide feedback on an instructional strategy. It can be helpful to know whether, and how, students perceive that strategies such as group work are helping their learning.

- Prompts to gain feedback about the materials and teaching. Questions can be devised to gain feedback for the teacher about their own actions/choices during the lesson. Although more risky from a teacher's point of view, they send out a message about the value the teacher places on his/her own learning.

One way in which exit tickets can be used is to provide input for the following lesson. Devise an exit ticket that requires students to reflect on the rationale of a particular individual under study. This may be a literary character, historic figure, politician, famous scientist preparing a particular experiment, engineer/mathematician performing calculations and so on. The exit ticket will pose a question about that individual's motivation or thought process. Students' responses will form the opening to a first draft of an essay.

A playful experimentation approach: mind mapping

Invented by Tony Buzan, the modern mind map is a powerful graphic technique using words, images, numbers, logic, rhythm, colour and spatial awareness to see connections, hierarchies and patterns between ideas (Buzan and Buzan, 1993). It is useful for planning, organising and as a memory prompt.

Tony Buzan suggests a few key principles for drawing a mind map.[4] Underlying each of these is the idea that the brain works most creatively when it has an interesting stimulus to look at, and less well when faced with many words. He suggests that you begin your mind map on a landscape-oriented blank sheet of paper and that you start in the centre. The space you create in this way avoids restricting the 'direction' of your thinking and, advises Buzan, it allows your brain to express itself more naturally. At the centre of your map should be an image rather than a word. This acts to stimulate and focus your mind, and colour (rather than plain black and white) will further 'energise' your thinking.

Associations between ideas are more easily developed in your mind – and remembered – if you use branches to connect your ideas to the central image, and then to connect lower-level concepts to those first-level ideas. Nothing should float alone unconnected. Buzan suggests these connecting branches are drawn curved rather than straight to keep your brain interested. If flexibility is desirable, single words should replace sentences. Finally, it is good practice to use images wherever possible, even replacing those single words. This cuts down on the number of words your memory needs to store.

This said, even if you do not want to use colour and graphics as extensively as Buzan suggests, it can still be a very useful way of organising ideas. At the

---

4 See http://www.tonybuzan.com/about/mind-mapping/.

Going Deeper

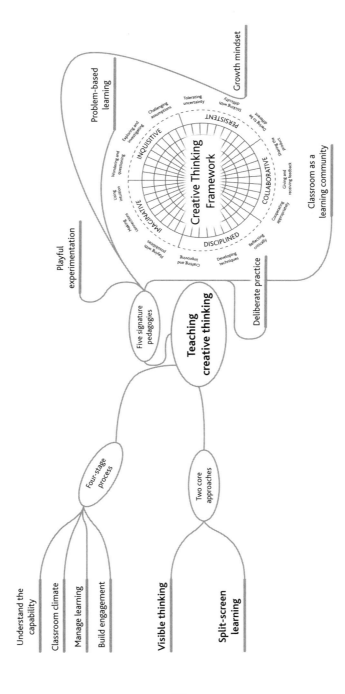

Mind map for teaching creative thinking

beginning of a course, key topics and concepts from the syllabus could be mapped visually around a central idea or concept. Students may be able to create this themselves from the syllabus or a template could be provided to which they can add and make connections as the course progresses. Linkages between topics in maths, for example, could help students to see connections that might be useful to them in solving problems and in understanding abstract concepts.

Whatever level you teach at you could use a mind map to:

- Outline the course you will be teaching and its content.
- Encourage pupils to brainstorm what they already know about a new topic you are starting.
- Help pupils to organise lines of argument after watching a film or reading an article.
- Act as a means of encouraging a group to work together by all contributing to one mind map about a topic of interest.

Engaging parents with the idea of creative thinking

What would perfect communication be like in a parent–teacher relationship? Ideally, both parties would share everything pertinent to a pupil's learning so that the other can reinforce and scaffold learning as needed. When it comes to creative thinking, this isn't simply about content. It's also about the capabilities we're trying to grow in children. Of course, we're not talking about separating subject matter learning and creative thinking, and neither is it helpful to report back purely on one side: 'teachers can develop *both* creative potential *and* students' knowledge' of subject matter simultaneously (Beghetto, 2010, p. 453).

A culture of creative thinking embedded across a school is a good reason for choosing the school in the first place! A school that truly values creative thinking will want to make sure that parents are on the same page. We know that for all the vital impact schools have on children, the most significant influence is their home life; parents and schools can work together with great success.

Parents need to know that they don't need to have experienced academic success themselves to ensure their own children experience it. What counts isn't academic knowledge but 'genuine interest and active engagement' (OECD, 2012, p. 3). The authors go on to list the forms of parental involvement that are most strongly related to student outcomes in PISA tests. These include: reading to children when they are young, engaging in discussions that promote critical thinking and setting a good example (for example, by reading for enjoyment). Note that of all the possible ways parents could interact with their children to improve outcomes, developing their critical thinking makes this list.

Critical thinking is encouraged at home as parents discuss 'complex' issues. This includes social or political issues – that is, real-world concerns rather than purely academic ones. Critical thinking develops in this reflective environment 'because discussing social or political issues motivates students to draw on information, make connections, summarise and communicate ideas effectively' (Borgonovi and Montt, 2012, p. 51).

For young children, a complex issue can be thinking through themes in their latest storybook: alternative endings, moral messages, what happens next, how else could the prince have climbed into Rapunzel's tower? A sad reality that many teachers face is that too many children don't have access to books in their homes. Accompanying children's 'book bags' home needs to be a guide for parents about how to help with reading. Many schools will send home a one-time guide, but the reminder needs to be more frequent – and without the assumption that parents either enjoy reading or know how to engage with it. Other schools invite parents into schools to walk them through reading and discussion strategies. Finding creative ways to draw in the least involved parents will always be a challenge, but a two-pronged approach is to teach children to question habitually the texts they take home, as well as to educate their parents.

Parents need to understand what schools mean by 'thinking creatively' and many will need 'reprogramming' from what Ronald Beghetto (2010, p. 455) calls the 'big-C bias', in which people 'come to believe that the only creativity that matters is at the most eminent level'. It's all too easy to undermine the notion that everyone can learn to be more creative when parents label one child (perhaps the dreamy one who likes colouring in) as the 'creative' or 'artistic' one (and this can be equally limiting to the so-called 'creative' one).

Some ways that schools can deter this bias include:

- Making the five dimensions (inquisitive, persistent, collaborative, disciplined, imaginative) visible.
- Talking about the five dimensions with parents.
- Inviting parents to assess their own strengths in each of the sub-habits.
- If teaching discrete subjects, demonstrating how each of the five dimensions come into play within subject areas: convince everyone of their equal value.

In *Educating Ruby* (2015), Guy Claxton and Bill Lucas came up with some simple practical ideas which schools might like to pass on to their parents. These include:

- Seeing the value of replacing 'I can't' with 'I can't yet' and taking opportunities to practise this.
- Actively spending time with children after watching TV to ask and answer questions about what you have been viewing.
- Playing the game of Crazy Connections (where you try to connect two highly unlikely items together) during mealtimes.
- Taking children to museums, galleries, historic houses, community events – anything which is likely to stimulate creative conversations.

Co-curricular experiences for creative thinking

There are many valuable lessons that just can't be taught within the time constraints of the school day. But it is often in out-of-school extended periods of activity that some of life's most important lessons are learned, classroom concepts are clarified, understanding is reinforced and emotional maturity is developed.

Sometimes it's the new environment. It might be the different way time is experienced, the break from routine or the irregular dynamics of pupil–teacher or even pupil–pupil interactions. Or perhaps a new experience opens up a way of learning something that just hadn't hit home before.

We have described the importance of teachers having an interest or hobby that inspires them to draw anecdotes from either the process of doing, the process of learning or some other pertinent point. But for children (as well as adults) there is enormous value in learning something new and persisting with it. Persistence is bound to bring struggles as well as successes. Experiencing hurdles and overcoming them is the surest way for learners to kindle and then cement an inner certainty that a growth mindset is worth having.

Angela Duckworth, researcher in the study of the 'grit' characteristic in learners (Duckworth et al., 2007), has a principle she uses in raising her own children – one that helps us to understand why these seemingly unrelated activities can be of huge benefit to children. Duckworth's 'Hard Thing Rule' (2016, pp. 241–242) applies to each member of her family, herself included:

1. Everyone has to do a 'hard thing'. A hard thing is something that requires daily deliberate practice, and so for parents this can be their job!

2. You can quit but only at a natural break (when the season is over, when the tuition payment is up) and after the time period you've committed to – never on a bad day when you lose a race, when it's inconvenient, when practice clashes with a sleepover or when the teacher shouts at you.

3. You choose your own hard thing.

4. At high school, you must do at least one activity for at least two years.

Why is this so important? Because children learn to see things through. Not only does that develop their grit, but the experience of getting better at an activity gives confidence that you *can* get better at learning.

Service learning

Service learning provides a structured means of developing fruitful partnerships between schools and their communities. Its balanced emphasis on both student learning and addressing the genuine needs of the community ensures mutual benefit. Precisely what form service learning takes will depend on a matching of learning goals with the needs of service recipients. Teachers can then plan course materials to supplement what takes place outside of the classroom, as well as facilitate application of those experiences back in the classroom for academic and personal development.

Working on real problems can enhance all sorts of capabilities, and, of course, creative thinking can be developed with the right opportunities. The skill of the teacher is in finding ways to combine service to the community with valuable learning opportunities. A simple litter-picking exercise could be turned into a science project as findings are analysed and reported back to the community. Pupils might play with the Six Thinking Hats to consider and reflect on some suggestions for pollution reduction.

Kelly Kuolt and colleagues give an example of how sixth grade pupils gained real-world experience of playing with possibilities, crafting and improving and sharing a product as they saw through a project to provide educational materials for a Head Start programme to support low-income families.[5]

Ron Berger's inspiring example of the town water study demonstrates how students learned to draft and redraft when the product was to be shared with a real audience. Students learned real discipline as they, and the community, took their work deadly seriously: 'the whole town, and lots of nervous families, were anxiously awaiting their findings' (Berger, 2003, p. 112).

---

5   See http://giftededucationcommunicator.com/gec-summer-2015/teaching-skills-through-service-learning/.

Where classroom-based teaching for state standards/curriculum targets ends and service learning begins is a blurred line. Inspiring teachers like Berger will incorporate real-world, community-based examples wherever they can as a vehicle through which the things that matter are learned.

Work placements

During compulsory schooling many students will have the chance to apply for work shadowing, work experience or a work placement, although in the UK this is no longer a statutory requirement. While these opportunities are primarily about increasing pupils' understanding of an area of work or a role they might consider for the future, they are also more general introductions to the workplace that can 'embed some of the real world skills' such as 'independence, interpersonal skills, organisation, time management etc.' (Ofsted, 2016, p. 12).

Some placements will naturally be more conducive to developing creative thinking capabilities. This might be one factor for schools to consider when developing links with local businesses and organisations for the purpose of work experience. While some schools will take on the burden of finding placements for pupils, it is often down to individual pupils to make those introductions. Many will find experience through family or known contacts and may have little opportunity to be choosy, and there are obvious implications for disadvantaged children (Ofsted, 2016).

Mindful of these limitations, teachers will want to help pupils extract the maximum learning from their placement experiences. Schools with 'enterprise' as a priority will tend to prepare pupils in advance with the application details, such as guidance on how to write a CV and a checklist of practicalities they should make themselves aware of (like what to wear and who to report to).[6] But a better approach would include mechanisms for thinking through with pupils some of the ways their placements might develop and evidence capabilities, for example:

- How creative thinking capabilities might be developed in the employment context.

---

6   There is an example here from the state of Victoria, Australia: http://www.education.vic.gov.au/school/teachers/teachingresources/careers/work/Pages/welldone.aspx.

- How creative thinking might be relevant to the role of others within the pupil's immediate working environment.

- How small opportunities might help pupils to demonstrate creative thinking.

When real job application processes frequently demand skills-based interviews, it is possible for students to seek out and gain experience to add to their repertoire of capability-based anecdotes, even in a couple of weeks.

Again, post-hoc evaluation is more likely to be carried out where enterprise is already a priority for schools and is embedded in the curriculum (Ofsted, 2016, p. 14). Yet it can help pupils to reflect on their experience in terms of the creative thinking opportunities it has afforded or even the capabilities developed. Reflecting critically on the experience and putting these things onto paper is likely to be a helpful exercise for pupils as they consider their next steps beyond school.

Volunteering

Ofsted's (2011) review of volunteering practices observed that the best settings foster close collaboration with businesses and other groups in the community. The most effective programmes were 'at least in part, shaped by individual young people and involved a level of risk and challenge' (ibid., p. 5). What didn't work so well was where opportunities were longstanding, repetitive ones 'where teachers spoon-fed students ideas rather than working with them to develop their own projects' (ibid., p. 6).

Just as with service learning, volunteering can be something that schools consider an 'add on' or more integrated with mainstream learning. Ofsted found that the most effective settings 'found creative ways of integrating volunteering within courses and "in-house" projects' (ibid., p. 6). Again, considering the opportunities afforded to aspects of creative thinking is a useful exercise for students. They will benefit from continuous reflection throughout the experience using approaches that encourage critical and creative thinking.

Trips

School trips are about providing powerful learning experiences outside of the everyday, as well as being social experiences for students. Because they place students in an environment where knowledge can be applied in the real world, trips are great opportunities for embedding creative thinking – provided they give students the chance to think for themselves about applying what they know. Creative thinking – that which goes beyond memorisation and recall – then 'not only enlivens what is learned but can also deepen student understanding' as students apply what they have learned (Beghetto, 2010, p. 453).

Trips can be educational or purely for fun. A trip might link to and bring alive a specific unit of work – for example, the English department might take its Year 10s to the Globe Theatre in London to see a Shakespeare play they are studying for GCSE, the examination used at 16+ in the UK. It might more overtly link the broad subject to competencies like social awareness and empathy – for example, the history department might take its biennial trip to Normandy's D-Day battlefields. Or it might provide opportunities for pupils to collect data for a specific project – for example, the geography department might do a local river study.

Some trips are very easily tied to specific aspects of creative thinking. Examples might be a creative writing workshop that looks at 'playing with possibilities', 'sticking with difficulty' and 'developing techniques', or a debating trip that clearly aims to develop 'making connections', 'daring to be different' and 'reflecting critically'. Other trips will require more forethought to link them to creative thinking. We would suggest that during the planning of any trip, teachers remind themselves of the different dimensions and sub-habits involved in creative thinking and think about how opportunities for experiencing these can be incorporated.

In this chapter we have explored some key principles of signature pedagogies for teaching creative thinking and, at the same time, looked more closely at specific methods for teaching the fifteen aspects of creative thinking we have suggested. Although we have linked methods to specific aspects, it is often the case that they work for several different ones – our ideas are indicative only. More broadly, we have looked at how different areas of practice within the school – from professional development to involvement of parents – can be given a creative thinking focus. In the next chapter we look at some promising practices that embrace and embed creative thinking in education.

Chapter 5
Promising Practices

Some case studies

> We are also convinced that schools exist to help develop the characters and attributes of young people, alongside their knowledge and understanding of the curriculum. For the last few years, we have been involved in research about the value of creative learning. Out of this research a set of Habits of Mind has emerged that appear to be associated with successful creative learners.
>
> Thomas Tallis School, London[1]

Across the world, schools are beginning to adopt the kind of ideas described in this book. Increasingly, national and state curricula are requiring schools to embrace creative thinking, as are international curricula (like the International Baccalaureate) and international assessments (such as PISA). Sometimes schools are doing it *despite* their national curriculum, national assessment or accountability frameworks.

In this chapter, we feature a number of promising school practices and then describe some international initiatives exploring creative thinking which provide a wider context. In each example we have tried to highlight specific aspects of their approach which might be of use to head teachers and teachers seeking inspiration, and to summarise the key learning points.

We also want schools to understand the degree to which a full engagement with the cultivation of capabilities, alongside knowledge and skills, means that schools end up making quite fundamental changes to their own organisation. We start with two secondary schools with which we have been collaborating for a number of years, Rooty Hill High School in Australia and Thomas Tallis School in England.

---

1 See http://www.thomastallisschool.com/tallis-habits.html.

Rooty Hill High School, Sydney – leadership, visible thinking routines, professional learning and technology

Rooty Hill High School is an extraordinary secondary school in the western suburbs of Sydney. Serving a catchment area which includes many families with low incomes, the school consistently educates its students to the highest standards, both in terms of conventional academic qualifications and the capabilities which its students demonstrate.

Over the past five years Rooty Hill has been using our five-dimensional model of creative thinking (see page 22) to inform its approach to curriculum planning, pedagogy and assessment. The Australian curriculum is different from many, certainly from the curricula of the four nations which make up the UK, in that it is framed in terms of capabilities as well as subjects. Australian schools are invited to focus on critical and creative thinking, personal and social capability, ethical understanding and intercultural understanding, as well as subjects like English, mathematics, science, music and history.

Under the leadership of its principal, Christine Cawsey, deputy principal, Conny Mattimore, and former principal, Dianne Hennessy, Rooty Hill has shown how it is possible to communicate their vision graphically and holistically to staff and students. A full-colour version of the model on page 121 appears on the inside front cover.

They have developed our original framework in three helpful ways:

1. Focusing on key verbs associated with each of the five habits. So, for example, inquisitive is associated with argue, deconstruct, examine, explore, identify, investigate, question and retrieve. This helps staff and students to be more aware of the vocabulary associated with a specific dimension and encourages them to use it within different subjects.

2. Being explicit about how each of the five dimensions create opportunities for students to practise supporting skills. So, looking at inquisitive again, this would include: (a) ask questions to form new ideas, (b) seek answers and research and (c) contest ideas and knowledge using knowledge.

ROOTY HILL HIGH SCHOOL
A Community School Committed to Excellence in Learning, Leadership and Achievement

THE CREATIVITY WHEEL

Imaginative
- Wondering & Questioning: ask questions to form new ideas?
- Exploring & Investigating: seek answers and research?
- Challenging Assumptions: contest ideas and knowledge using knowledge?
- Making Connections: link ideas for new connections?
- Using Intuition: predict and follow up?
- Playing with Possibilities: think outside the box?

Verbs (Imaginative/Inquisitive center): design, experiment, formulate, hypothesise, invent, propose, reconstruct, speculate / argue, deconstruct, examine, explore, identify, investigate, question, retrieve

Inquisitive
Visible thinking routines (outer ring, top): Claim-support-question • See-think-wonder • Zoom in • Chalk talk • Connect-extend-challenge • What makes you say that? • Headings • Think-puzzle-explore • Compass points • I used to think... now I think • 4 Cs • Red light, yellow light

Visible thinking routines (outer ring, upper left): Claim-support-question • See-think-wonder • Red light, yellow light • Circle of viewpoints • The explanation game • Step inside • Generate-sort-connect-elaborate • Zoom in • CSI: colour, symbol, image • Headlines

Persistent
- Tolerating Uncertainty: work in an unstructured way?
- Sticking with Difficulty: find better, smarter or more creative ideas?
- Daring to be Different: take risks with their thinking?

Verbs (Persistent/Collaborative center): create, invent, interrogate, predict, presume, re-assess, review, suppose / appraise, check, collaborate, consult, critique, demonstrate, explain, model

Disciplined
- Crafting & Improving: value effort and progress?
- Developing Techniques: practise skills?
- Reflecting Critically: evaluate personal performance?

Verbs (Disciplined center): assess, justify, practice, question, reconsider, rehearse, repeat, test

Visible thinking routines (outer ring, lower left): Compass points • I used to think... now I think • Explanation game • Step inside • Connect-extend-challenge • What makes you say that? • Headlines • 3-2-1 Bridge

Collaborative
- Cooperating Appropriately: be an asset to teams?
- Giving and Receiving Feedback: critique each other's work?
- Sharing the Product: share creative products with others?

Visible thinking routines (outer ring, right): Tug-of-war • Generate-sort-connect-elaborate • 4 Cs • Think-puzzle-explore • Circle of viewpoints • Microlab protocol • Connect-extend-challenge • What makes you say that? • Zoom in

Visible thinking routines (outer ring, bottom): Microlab protocol • Chalk talk • Think-pair-share • Sentence-phrase-word • Generate-sort-connect-elaborate • Compass points • Circle of viewpoints • Zoom in

THE LEGEND
- Verbs
- Creativity disposition
- Creativity sub-disposition
- In our programs and our practices do we provide opportunities for students to ...
- Visible thinking routine

Developed by Rooty Hill High School from the work of Lucas, Claxton and Spencer.

3. Incorporating many of Project Zero's thinking routines (see Chapter 2) to help staff and students learn simple procedures to make the five habits a normal part of their learning.[2] Rooty Hill have adapted our framework to list relevant thinking routines under each of the five broad habits. For example, thinking routines that might be useful for developing 'inquisitive' learners include:

- See–think–wonder: A visible thinking routine that encourages students to make careful observations and considered interpretations of what they see.

- Zoom in: Part of an image is shown and students are asked to think about what they are seeing and what questions they have before the image is zoomed out to reveal more detail. Students are asked what new things they can see, whether the new information has answered any of their questions and what new things they are wondering about. This routine helps turn students' self-talk into metacognitive thinking, as they learn to suspend judgement and make educated predictions. It also helps them to learn that new information can change their original hypothesis.

- Chalk talk: As a thinking routine (described further in Ritchhart et al., 2011), chalk talk gives each student the chance to express their thoughts and be heard. Chalk talk is silent; it's a conversation on paper that takes place as the students pose questions, wonder and link responses to their peers' using markers (or chalk!). The paper can be preserved for later reflection.

- Connect–extend–challenge: Individuals, small groups or whole classes use this thinking routine for connecting new ideas to prior knowledge. It involves collecting and recording students' thoughts on the three issues: connect (how do the new ideas connect to what you already know?), extend (what new ideas did you come across that extend your existing thinking?) and challenge (what new questions/confusions/gaps in your knowledge can you now identify?).

---

2 For more information about these thinking routines and others see: http://www.pz.harvard.edu.

- What makes you say that? This routine promotes evidence-based reasoning as students are asked, 'What's going on?' and 'What do you see that makes you say that?' This can work with artefacts as well as pieces of text and concepts.

- Think–puzzle–explore: A routine that is helpful at the beginning of a topic to start students thinking about how their existing knowledge might stimulate deeper enquiry. They are asked to think (about what they know), to consider questions still in their minds (puzzle) and – often after discussing think and puzzle as a group – to ponder how they might further explore the topic.

- Compass points: This is a routine for examining propositions and thinking about how to express an opinion on them. Beginning with group discussion, responses can be classified into four categories (N = need to know, E = excited, S = stance (or suggestion for moving forward) or W = worrisome) and recorded for all to see. Students can build on one another's ideas and consider how their own thinking has changed.

- Headlines: A routine for summarising ideas into a key concept that involves writing a newspaper-type headline to sum up the most important aspect of an issue. Students can reflect upon how their thinking on a topic changes as they compare the headlines they write over time.

- Claim–support–question. This routine is used for clarifying truth claims. Students make a claim about the facts of an aspect of a topic. They support their claim with statements about what they know/see/feel. They then pose a question about what is still unexplained.

- I used to think … Now I think … This is a routine that you might use if you want students to remember a particular topic or concept. In considering their responses to these two openings, students can reflect on how their thinking has changed, and why. This develops their ability to reason using cause-and-effect relationships.

- 4 Cs: This routine helps learners to engage with a text in a structured way. It asks them to make *connections* (between the text and their life/learning outside – like our starter idea, 'What does this remind you of?'), to *challenge* (the ideas or assumptions in the text), to ask themselves what key *concepts* they think are most important and to think about *changes* in attitude or action that the text provokes.

- Red light, yellow light: This is a thinking routine that helps students to be on the lookout for 'puzzles of truth'. These are signs that indicate there may be truth issues within a text. Students read selected material and look for 'red lights' (things that make them want to stop and question/explore further) and for 'yellow lights' (things that make them want to proceed with caution). They note the page number and their reasoning for later discussion. These puzzles of truth may be logical fallacies, weak arguments, one-sided arguments, appeals to emotion, broad generalisations or lack of expertise, for example.

By developing our thinking in this way, Rooty Hill has made it really easy for staff and students to get started, and also demonstrated their own creativity in the process. Reflecting on their approach, Christine Cawsey identifies three important aspects of their journey.

1. The identification of lead faculties and project leaders

When the school has a major project to do, its teachers identify lead faculties – teams of teachers who will conduct small-scale trials and evaluations of platforms and tools they think will be effective. Where they are effective, they are adopted across the school. The school also creates 'positions' within faculties for teachers who are peer leaders and coaches for projects within the school plan.

2. The creation of professional learning teams

At Rooty Hill, all teachers (including the principals and senior executive staff) belong to a professional learning team and undertake action research into a targeted area identified in the school plan. Members of each team design and conduct action research that informs the outputs or 'products' of the professional learning teams during or at the end of the year, which are then adopted by the whole school. The school uses the model of action research developed by the Expansive Education Network.

3. Deliberately building a capability-driven curriculum

In New South Wales, the curriculum has traditionally been driven by strong content frameworks and there has been a tension in secondary schools between traditional 'content-based' approaches to each subject and the capabilities that are assessed in national examinations, such as NAPLAN (National Assessment Program – Literacy and Numeracy). Working with the Centre for Real-World Learning at the University of Winchester and three in-house consultants, the school has reframed its subject-based programming and lesson design to 'teach through the ACARA capabilities'.[3] Most recently, this has enabled the school to pilot new approaches to the assessment of capabilities.

Rooty Hill High School was recently recognised by the Global Education Leaders' Partnership as an innovative twenty-first century school.[4] In particular, the school's PERSIST values (participation and enthusiasm; excellence; respect and responsibility; success; innovation and creativity; safety; teamwork) and the exciting work being done to underpin all learning with capabilities was mentioned in the Global Education Leaders' Partnership report to the New South Wales Minister for Education. *The Educator Magazine* recognised Rooty Hill High School as one of the forty most innovative schools in Australia in 2016.

---

3   For more on the Australian Curriculum Assessment and Reporting Authority's general capabilities see: http://www.acara.edu.au/curriculum/general-capabilities.
4   The Global Education Leaders' Partnership (GELP) is an international alliance of education leaders and consultants that aims to transform education of the future. For more information see: http://gelponline.org/.

Key learning points

Rooty Hill High School aims to embed creative thinking into the school in five ways, which are reflected in these key learning points:

1. Invest in clear communication with staff, students and parents.
2. Identify and support project leaders to test and trial ideas using action research.
3. Create a professional learning community which is seen as having a high status.
4. Map capabilities (such as creative thinking) against the school's curriculum and give staff practical ideas for getting started.
5. Track the progress of student capability using digital portfolios.

Thomas Tallis School, London – leadership, whole-school integration and pedagogy

Wherever you are in Thomas Tallis School you are rarely far away from the poster featured on page 127. You'll recognise its content as it is a version of our five-dimensional creative thinking model (see page 22). In 2011, as a result of a commission from Creativity, Culture and Education, we (with Guy Claxton) started to work with Thomas Tallis and ten other schools to explore ways of cultivating and assessing creativity in schools. Since then we have continued to learn from their innovative practices and they have consciously sought to undertake their own enquiries as part of the Expansive Education Network.

Promising Practices

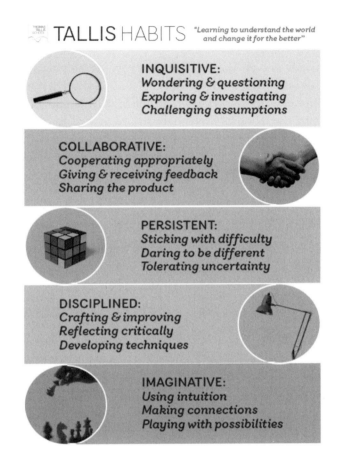

Thomas Tallis sees itself as a community of scholars who support each other to be inquisitive, persistent, collaborative, disciplined and imaginative. Their posters with these five habits and their associated icons are a confident expression of the importance of these creative habits, just as the school timetable is an expression of the important disciplinary subjects which make up students' schedules.

The school cultivates the habits across the curriculum with a habits focus each half term. Students have opportunities to self-assess their progress against the habits, with some subject areas using the habits as a basis for assessment at Key Stage 3.

There is no contradiction at Thomas Tallis between developing students' creative habits of mind and their knowledge of specific disciplines. They are embedded in all that the school does, both formally and informally. Unlike other curriculum mapping attempts, the Thomas Tallis habits have proved to be very effective in developing a shared language among colleagues and students with which to talk about creativity. However, there is no immediate or exclusive link to the arts, for example; these particular habits of mind are as desirable in science as they are in music.

Some of the ways in which this is achieved include:

- Building opportunities to explicitly develop creative habits of mind into schemes of work and lesson planning (split-screen teaching across the school).

- Foregrounding particular creative habits of mind in lesson starters and plenaries (as we suggested in Chapter 4).

- Developing the Tallis Pedagogy Toolkit of the kinds of teaching and learning methods which are most likely to cultivate the five creative habits of mind (many of which are similar to the suggestions in this book).

- Developing opportunities for students to engage in extended learning enquiries in order to exercise a range of learning habits.

- Using a web app called Tallis Habits within Year 7 computer science lessons to encourage students to reflect on their learning habits.[5]

- Rewarding students in Years 7 and 8 for demonstrating progress in acquiring Tallis Habits and reporting this progress to parents.

- Conducting action research about the impact of Tallis Habits across the curriculum, supported by the Expansive Education Network and the University of Greenwich.

---

5 See https://tallishabits.herokuapp.com/flock.

Recently, the school has built on pioneering developmental work undertaken by Rooty Hill High School (the previous case study) and created a model which shows how habits can be linked to the kinds of learning methods most likely to cultivate them.[6] Rooty Hill is featured again in the next chapter where we explore assessment issues.

Key learning points

Thomas Tallis aims to embed creativity across the school in six ways which are reflected in these key learning points:

1. Invest in clear communication with staff, students and parents.

2. Stress the equal importance of disciplinary knowledge and capabilities such as critical thinking.

3. Highlight different dimensions of the Tallis Habits each half term.

4. Focus on the teaching and learning methods likely to cultivate the Tallis Habits.

5. Actively promote teacher enquiry as a means of building professional capability.

6. Build feedback about creative habits into whole-school assessment and reporting.

---

6 Thomas Tallis School's 'Tallis Habits Pedagogy Wheel', alongside details of each of the teaching strategies, is available at: http://www.thomastallisschool.com/tallis-pedagogy-wheel-guide.html.

Redlands Primary School, Reading – growth mindsets, enquiry-based learning and the University of Redlands degree courses

Redlands Primary School in Reading, England, sees creative thinking as one of the core skills and attitudes that children need in an ever-changing and globally connected world. Its ethnically diverse community is seen as a source of strength – one that fosters understanding of the unique strengths and richness of others' ideas and ways of thinking.

At Redlands, the explicit focus on creative learning is evidenced in its values and vision. It is embedded through the school in three key ways. First, it is working to foster a growth mindset culture. Teaching and learning is conducted in such a way that children and adults understand that in order to learn they must be brave and make mistakes, and this allows them to tackle challenges they wouldn't have attempted before. The sorts of approaches to teaching that develop a growth mindset in children give them the ability to question, enjoy challenge, embrace failure, explore and show resilience. Each of these elements involves learning to think creatively. Redlands works to foster these skills and aptitudes because a growth mindset equips them for bright futures.

Second, Redlands fosters a topic-based enquiry approach, encouraging the children to ask questions and challenge ideas. Clear guidelines and ground rules are established early on in the children's educational journey at Redlands so they learn to question and challenge in a sensitive and respectful way. The result is that children come to realise that one question very often leads to another and that a journey of discovery inevitably follows. The teacher adopts the role of facilitator, similar to that in a Philosophy for Children context, providing a forum which supports the enquiry and a creative thinking approach.

Third, Redlands fosters a creative thinking/learning culture via its University of Redlands 'degree courses'. In the second half of the summer term, the children are given a prospectus from which they can select a course in an area beyond what the curriculum can offer. All members of staff are involved in teaching the courses, and the courses offered play to individuals' personal strengths and interests. Some examples of past courses include bicycle maintenance, go-kart building, camping skills, horticulture, animal care, fashion, hospitality and catering, dramatic arts, felt and paper making and many more. Children work in mixed year groups one morning per week to learn a host of new skills – practical, intellectual, personal and social. This experience enhances their sense of aspiration and opens their eyes to a wider world. Creative thinking forms a fundamental part of this experience as the children are presented with a range of problem-solving scenarios depending on the course they have opted for.

Here is the 2016 course prospectus to give you an idea of the kinds of things which might be on offer:

University of Redlands' 'degree course' prospectus

Title of course	Year groups							
	Foundation Stage 2	1	2	3	4	5	6
Bags Galore!					✓	✓	✓
Felt and Paper Making						✓	✓
Scrapheap Challenge					✓	✓	✓
Craft Crazee				✓	✓	✓	✓
International Art and Craft	✓	✓	✓				
The Seaside	✓	✓	✓				
Redlands: Around the World	✓	✓	✓	✓			
Bicycle Maintenance						✓	✓
Floury Fingers						✓	✓
Doggy Daycare				✓	✓	✓	✓

Title of course	Year groups						
	Foundation Stage 2	1	2	3	4	5	6
Healthy Body, Healthy Mind	✓	✓	✓				
Nuts about Netball						✓	✓
'Come on, you Redlanders!'			✓	✓			
Powerful Polish		✓	✓	✓			
Fun French	✓	✓	✓				
Holly Bolly				✓	✓	✓	✓
Film Making				✓	✓	✓	✓
Dramatic Arts	✓	✓	✓				

Through these three approaches, Redlands ensures that creative learning is at the heart of its practice, which is further enriched by links with the school's community and other partnerships. Children are constantly encouraged to:

- Take ownership of and direct their learning.
- Question and challenge.
- Make connections and see relationships.
- Envisage what might be.
- Explore ideas and be open-minded.
- Reflect critically on ideas, actions and outcomes.
- Think independently.
- Embrace new challenges and experiences.

- View mistakes as being at the root of good learning.
- Regard the learning process as incremental – 'I am not able to do this … yet.'
- Be brave and resilient learners.

The school makes these opportunities available by offering:

- A child-led curriculum. Finding out what the children already know, immersing them in the subject matter and finding out what they want to learn.
- Opportunities to explore and generate questions through open-ended tasks and problem-solving activities.
- Flexibility with planning which means that the teachers may not know which direction the learning is going to go in.
- A range of learning experiences both within and outside the school.
- A values-led approach with social, moral, spiritual and cultural development at the core.
- Cross-phase learning opportunities which develop children's social skills and their understanding and appreciation of others.
- A diverse school community with over forty languages spoken – this encourages empathy, respect and tolerance (which support aspects of creative learning so well).

Key learning points

Redlands aims to embed creative thinking into the school in four ways, which are reflected in these key learning points:

1. Underpin all learning by embedding a growth mindset approach across the school.

2. Use rigorous topic-based enquiry approaches, supported by Philosophy for Children techniques.

3. Consciously seek to extend children's horizons.

4. Encourage children to take responsibility for their own learning by becoming more critical and reflective.

Brunswick East Primary School, Melbourne – multi-age learning communities, thinking routines and Philosophy for Children

Brunswick East Primary School (BEPS) is in the inner suburbs of Melbourne, Australia. It specifically values philosophical enquiry and a sense of curiosity. Students and teachers work together in multi-age Learning Communities of Foundation, Grades 123 and Grades 456. Its website expands this in more detail:

> Here at BEPS students and teachers work together as communities of learners, in fact our class organisation is based around mixed-age groupings in flexible 'Learning Communities' with core 'Home Groups'. Children learn best when the learning is shared through collaborative inquiry, which develops a strong sense of belonging and connection to community.
>
> A focus on philosophical thinking in 'communities of inquiry' for many years at BEPS has created an ethos of deep thinking, exploration of big ideas and grappling with challenges and possibilities. This process promotes critical thinking and requires that members of the group show respect for each other.
>
> Children work in small groups to engage in collaborative investigation and discussion, constructing understandings, skills, and knowledge shared by the group. Each individual child in a group will then refine their own world view and create new knowledge. Within a community children learn to listen and communicate respectfully; to challenge and extend their own thinking and that of others; and to gain social confidence and the courage to speak out about things that matter to them.[7]

---

7   See http://beps.vic.edu.au/learning/learning-communities/.

BEPS is influenced by several theories of learning: constructivism, Dewey and Reggio Emilia, and on its website quotes Loris Malaguzzi (one of the Reggio Emilia founders) to support its practices: 'Learning and teaching should not stand on opposite banks and just watch the river flow by; instead, they should embark together on a journey down the water. Through an active, reciprocal exchange, teaching can strengthen learning how to learn' (Malaguzzi, 1998, p. 83).

Australia's capability-led national curriculum has recently been further developed by the Victorian Curriculum and Assessment Authority (VCAA) so that it can be embedded within and across the curriculum and, from 2017 onwards, reliably assessed. Along with ten other schools from across the state of Victoria, BEPS joined a professional learning community of schools, supported by the Centre for Real-World Learning, in an action research project to explore different ways of undertaking this.

BEPS chose to focus on two of the VCAA capabilities: ethical understanding and critical and creative thinking. Within the school, each learning community developed an enquiry around a big concept to explore the teaching and assessing of the two capabilities. One learning community developed an enquiry to explore the concept: human history is the history of ingenuity, innovation and invention. The essential questions developed by the learning community team included:

- How has science shaped our world?
- In what ways do humans organise history?
- How do innovations affect our world?
- What was an innovation that changed the course of history?
- Who has contributed to the advancement of science?
- How have inventions changed our lives (e.g. work, leisure, culture)?
- How have inventions changed the course of history?
- How do humans decide if an invention has had a positive influence on our society?

This enquiry ran for two semesters and was supported by weekly philosophy sessions to develop ethical understandings of the topic and teach critical and creative thinking skills.

Another community of enquiry discussion topic was animal testing which asked questions such as: what are all of the possible opinions that people may have about animal testing? What evidence or reasons might they have for these opinions? The learning intention was: I can examine how problems may contain more than one ethical issue. The teaching team also used thinking routines to support the enquiry and to make student thinking visible. These thinking routines were often used as evidence of understanding and were moderated in weekly team meetings.

After another learning community visited the National Gallery of Victoria, they used the thinking routine see–think–wonder to give a structure for the students to share their understanding of the exhibition they had visited, develop ideas and further their enquiry into diversity.

As part of its work with VCAA and the Centre for Real-World Learning, BEPS has specifically tried to use the continuum mapping developed by VCAA showing different levels of progress within the critical and creative thinking capability. To do this they have undertaken a range of teacher moderation activities looking at different examples of students' learning and starting to give levels to pupils' work.

In their work on thinking routines, BEPS has drawn on the work of Ron Ritchhart (2004) and his exploration of intellectual character. For their recent action research, each teaching team explored one of the eight cultural forces that shape culture: expectations, language, time, modelling, opportunities, routines, interactions and environment.

Jill Howells, a key leader of the work described in this case study, reflecting on the impact of the introduction of Philosophy for Children, told us: 'Students learn how to question, make connections and think deeply about their thinking. They also learn how to listen to one another, take turns and work collaboratively.'

Key learning points

BEPS embeds critical and creative thinking into the school in the following ways:

1. Organises the school into multi-age learning communities.
2. Uses enquiry-based learning.
3. Develops and embeds an ethos of Philosophy for Children across the school.
4. Uses visible thinking routines.
5. Listens respectfully to children and values their thinking to develop a love of learning, critical and creative thinking and ability to identify and respond to ethical issues.

Our Lady of Victories Primary, Keighley – skills-led curriculum, sense of adventure and themed 'wonder weeks'

Our Lady of Victories School describes itself as a school of creativity with a creative curriculum. Learning is skills based and theme led. Mornings are relatively traditional and are largely made up of numeracy and literacy lessons to ensure the basic skills are covered and afternoon lessons are based on a theme.

Our Lady of Victories believes that education should be an adventure, with all children having opportunities to experience wonder and awe. Its head teacher, John Devlin, is passionate in his conviction that primary schools have much to learn from Early Years education, especially in the way they deliberately try to build on the interests of the children.

This principle extends to staff too, who are encouraged to create 'wonder weeks' once a term. A wonder week is a themed week, the theme of which can be decided by the teacher or the children. Recent examples include horse riding, the Beatles, football, Japan, pottery and playing the guitar. The teachers plan activities and experiences using a planning grid, which ensures that provision connects explicitly with the national curriculum at the same time as being creative and cross-curricular in its nature.

The school identifies themes which are broad enough to encourage creative thinking in many different subjects. Two recent examples are 'I wonder' and 'Through the window'. There is a particular commitment to residential trips, typically to Scotland, France or Holland. The class will present their work to the school and community and share their experiences. They are encouraged to use a range of media – such as Photo Story 3, PowerPoint and podcasting – uploading work onto the school's virtual learning environment.

The school's focus is on the cultivation of creative skills of the kind described in our creative thinking model on page 22. Pupils are encouraged to keep creative learning journals to reflect on their experiences. They are also rewarded with creative stickers when they achieve significant progress in, for example, areas of curiosity, cooperation and problem-solving.

 Showing curiosity and investigating objects.

 Working as part of a team (cooperation).

 Finding ways to solve problems.

Our Lady of Victories' 'creative stickers'

The school has run its own radio station, Radio LV, for ten years. Every Friday at 3 p.m., Radio LV is on air providing an authentic audience for the children's work and a powerful way of engaging with parents and local people. Then they make a podcast of the show which is uploaded to their website for people to listen to later.

Each show is made up of jokes, news, reports from school trips, poems, songs and interviews with staff, visitors and even celebrities. As well as being an obviously enjoyable and creative activity for a school to do while building confidence in the children, the school has noticed significant improvements in both oracy and ICT.

Next on Our Lady of Victories School's to-do list is to start assessing children's progress in the development of creative thinking skills.

Key learning points

Our Lady of Victories aims to embed creative thinking into the school in four ways, which are reflected in these key learning points:

1. Go with the grain of children's interests.

2. Harness the passions of staff as you plan interdisciplinary work.

3. Take every opportunity to use Early Years principles and create extended periods of learning.

4. Provide authentic audiences for children's work whenever you can.

Duloe Church of England School, Liskeard – creative cross-curricular connections and teachers supported to take risks

Duloe Primary School was selected along with fifty-four others as a 'School of Creativity' as part of the Creative Partnerships programme.[8] Although the programme has now ceased, Duloe continues to describe itself as a School of Creativity, demonstrating its ongoing focus on creative teaching and learning. Its strapline is 'An adventure for the mind, and a home for the heart'. The school talks of 'working closely with each family and its local community to extend opportunities for creative learning and cater for individual needs, interests and enthusiasms'. For more than thirteen years, Duloe has actively sought to provide

---

8   Creative Partnerships, the UK's 'flagship creative learning programme', ran in England from 2002 until 2011. Schools that had already demonstrated outstanding practice in creative teaching and learning were selected to support a local network of schools, as well as to influence schools at a national level. See http://creative-partnerships.com/schools-of-creativity/.

exactly what they believe their children will benefit from, at the same time as ensuring that staff are constantly reinvigorated by supportive practices which give them confidence in their own professional knowledge and judgement.

This shows up in the way that teachers are given the freedom to be resourceful and take risks. Duloe staff are encouraged to create individual plans specific to class structures and to suit individual teachers' knowledge of their pupils' needs. There is a strong expectation that delivery of the curriculum will be innovative and expansive in every class, therefore pedagogy becomes more vibrant and exciting as staff take more 'risks' with their pupils' learning opportunities.

In terms of creative thinking, Duloe aims to provide a variety of opportunities that:

- Give pupils challenge and responsibility so they are stimulated to make progress as confident, resourceful, enquiring and independent learners. Responsibility for their own learning is developed at a very early age through planned opportunities for discussion such as plan–do–review sessions in Reception through to Duloe's 'learning detectives' in Years 5 and 6 . These pupils undertake peer monitoring and evaluation of learning across the school. Children soon learn that their thoughts and suggestions are taken seriously and acted upon within the class setting.

- Make creative links between areas of learning. Pupils are given the skills to face challenges in their learning and to develop a can-do approach. A class recently struggled with developing their writing skills to describe stories set on a riverbank. A suggestion from a child to walk outside resulted in a whole session of using their senses and visualisation skills, and the playground became the 'word bank' available for the children to refer to for the rest of the day. The resulting work was outstanding with links between many areas made explicit to the children.

Duloe adopts a whole-school themed approach to its curriculum which requires collaboration among staff. During each term, one day a week is designated for the exploration of whole-school themes. A recent example was, 'How would we survive as Stone Age man?' Reception and Year 1 'lived' outside for the whole day each week. The experience of lighting fires, collecting water, foraging and keeping warm gave them first-hand experience of what life may have been like. Other groups made paint from the natural materials on hand, used a large pestle and mortar (made by a parent from a tree trunk!) and cooked using foraged ingredients and the fire lit by the Reception group. Other sessions involved making pop-up books to illustrate life during Stone Age times and discussing the research undertaken in school and at home during the rest of the week. The children made pottery houses and also composed music to accompany their own dances.

During these 'creative days' the children are organised in cross-phase groups mixed from Year 2 to Year 6, with Reception and Year 1 if appropriate. Over a six-week period, the children experience at least five aspects of learning in subjects such as design and technology, ICT, dance, music, visual arts and sculpture.

A recent group activity on storytelling prepared backdrops for a school production. Links were made to mathematics using measurement and scale, ICT through photographic transfer and literacy by examining the roots of a variety of stories from around the world. The school often works towards final 'celebration afternoons' during which each mixed-phase group has to explain their working procedures, the development of ideas and how their work was interlinked.

In delivering their thematic teaching, there is a strong emphasis on promoting staff to be resourceful, to take risks and, above all, to enjoy their teaching activities. The school has built up a bank of rigorously planned and evaluated materials for delivering whole-school themes.

As a School of Creativity, Duloe has had the benefit of working with other schools nationally and with numerous practitioners. Staff have also worked closely with experts from the University of Exeter to help them to evaluate the impact of their practices on pupils and staff. Following one major project with a number of practitioners, a member of staff told us:

> The children have gone from strength to strength; they work and perform with great confidence and great ease, they're really comfortable with what they're doing and their sense of group awareness and group timing is outstanding for children their age. The benefits of this project have carried through into all areas of the curriculum and their learning.

In Chapter 4, we suggested that one way of embedding creative thinking more systematically is through the engagement of parents. One of Duloe's principal areas of focus is its conscious attempt to include families and the community in the school's learning and development. A powerful indication of the success Duloe has had with this approach was when a group of parents asked to run their own 'creative day'. Parents recognised their own skills and the opportunity for creative thinking that this would provide for the pupils. This joint involvement was a huge success and allowed all stakeholders to collaborate and enhance the experience for pupils.

Another theme of the school's work is expanding educational horizons. It aims to broaden children's thinking by facilitating several external visits during the school year for every child, as well as extending beyond the school by creating opportunities led by outside agencies. Duloe believes in providing an extremely high number of external visits each term for every class. The beauty of a small school is the flexibility it has; staff often jump at chances that come their way with little time for organisation and planning. The school has an extremely tight budget but staff often take opportunities that involve little cost or subsidy. The governing body wholeheartedly agrees with funding being used to enhance the pupils' learning in this way. Every school trip is subsidised to a lesser or greater degree due to the general circumstances of families.

Duloe's work with numerous outside partners has benefited from being very proactive and this has enhanced the opportunities with which the school has been involved. For example, a visiting actor who was able to role play as a Roman centurion was very happy to be asked to set up camp in the local woodland. The whole school – which over several weeks had all sewn and made their own Roman costumes – marched into the woods where they suddenly found an encampment with 'real-life' Roman soldiers and Celtic workers. The day was led by the questions, dialogue and responses of the children 'in the moment'. All parties were happy to follow this approach and run with the thinking and enquiry that ensued during the day.

Key learning points

Duloe aims to embed creative thinking into the school in six ways, which are reflected in these key learning points:

1. Commit to rigorously planned thematic work alongside subject-based delivery.
2. Help children to make connections and see relationships between subject areas.
3. Keep an open-minded approach in order to question and challenge effectively.
4. Trust teachers and support staff to take risks.
5. Actively engage with parents and families.
6. Promote a forward-thinking approach from all those involved with children's education, envisage what might be and keep options open.

From these case studies it is clear that individual schools, in these examples based in England and Australia, are showing how it is possible to put creative thinking at the heart of children's educational experiences in very different national contexts. In England, the government's current attention is focused on achievement, which is far more narrowly defined in terms of core academic subjects and what it calls an English Baccalaureate or EBacc. By contrast, Australia, where the federal government sets the framework and states choose how to implement it, is explicitly promoting capabilities such as creative thinking.

It is (sadly) England which is lagging behind international thinking with regard to the importance of creative thinking and other important capabilities. In the last part of this chapter, we review a few of the international and national initiatives which are focusing on creative thinking.

OECD, France – PISA domains, understanding pedagogy and assessing progression in critical and creative thinking skills

The Organisation for Economic Co-operation and Development is leading a shift in the way national education departments regard creative thinking in two ways. First, through its PISA tests, it is lending its authority to the importance of developing young people's capabilities. Second, it is undertaking research across fourteen countries, based on our five-dimensional model of creative thinking, using our five-dimensional framework as its starting point.

PISA tests

Every three years, as well as English, maths and science, PISA tests a fourth area, what it calls the 'innovative assessment domain'. In 2015 this was collaborative problem-solving and in 2018 it is global competence. In 2021 the focus will be on the topic of this book, creative thinking, using our five-dimensional framework as its starting point.

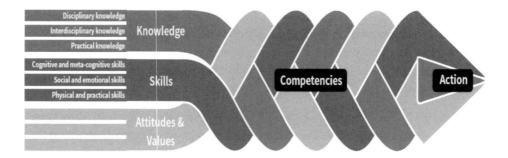

OECD 2030 framework for education

Source: OECD (2016, p. 2)

As it plans ahead to 2030, the OECD is developing a model of education (see page 144) which shows knowledge, skills, attitudes and values as inextricably intertwined. The outcome of this is the development of what the OECD calls 'competencies', a word which is pretty much synonymous with what we have called 'capabilities'.

OECD research into critical and creative thinking skills

Our model of creative thinking was published by the OECD in 2013: 'Progression in Student Creativity in School: First Steps Towards New Forms of Formative Assessments' (Lucas et al., 2013b) and has been the inspiration for an international research project to understand more about how creative thinking can best be cultivated and assessed.[9] A group of twelve countries with very different education systems are undertaking this research: Brazil, China, Finland, France, Hungary, India, Italy, the Netherlands, Slovak Republic, Thailand, the USA and Wales. The good news is that, across very different cultures, creative thinking is increasingly being valued. As OECD senior analyst Stéphan Vincent-Lancrin (2013) puts it:

> Are we really serious when we say that schools should nurture creativity and other skills for innovation? An increasing number of countries see fostering of creativity and critical thinking as the next educational challenge: traditional good grades may no longer suffice to equip the workforce with the skills needed to fuel innovation-driven economic growth.

There is also a growing consensus about the principles governing selection of the best pedagogies to teach it. These would seem to:

+ Be explicitly selected to produce desired outcomes.

+ Create opportunities for teachers to model desired habits of mind.

+ Make space for activities which are curious, authentic, extended in length, beyond school, collaborative and reflective.

---

9   See https://www.oecd.org/fr/sites/educeri/
assessingprogressionincreativeandcriticalthinkingskillsineducation.htm.

- Use signature pedagogies drawn from broad approaches such as: problem-based learning, growth mindset, classroom as a learning community, deliberate practice and playful experimentation.

- Make habits of mind and creative processes visible and valued.

- Actively engage students as co-designers.

- Integrate a range of assessment practices within teaching.

- Leave space for the unexpected.[10]

And, while we are less advanced in thinking about the assessment of creative thinking than we are its pedagogies, there is a growing understanding which we explore in the next chapter.

Key learning points

From the OECD work the following learning points are important:

1. Capabilities or competencies are a mixture of knowledge, skills, attitudes and values.

2. The student role as co-designer is important.

3. Assessment needs to be clearly integrated with teaching.

4. It helps when teachers leave space for the unexpected.

---

10 These principles were collaboratively developed in 2017 by Bill Lucas and participants from the twelve countries.

Victorian Curriculum and Assessment Authority, Australia – support for schools to develop signature pedagogies and innovative approaches to assessment of capabilities

The Victorian Curriculum and Assessment Authority (VCAA) is, arguably, leading the world in its approach to developing capabilities in its young people. It starts from a position of strength in that the Australian curriculum explicitly describes a capability called 'critical and creative thinking', which is conceptually very similar to creative thinking.

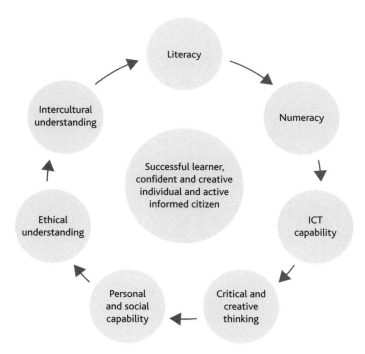

General capabilities in the Australian curriculum

Source: Australian Curriculum

As defined in the Australian curriculum, critical and creative thinking has four elements:

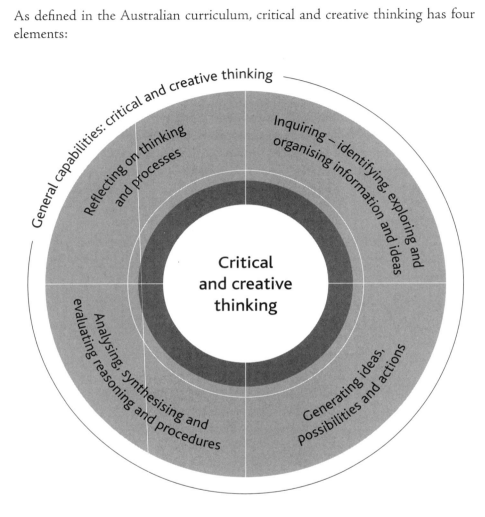

Critical and creative thinking in the Australian curriculum

Source: Australian Curriculum

VCAA has gone three stages further than specified by the Australian curriculum. First, it has chosen to simplify the four elements down to three strands: questions and possibilities, reasoning and metacognition.

The questions and possibilities strand supports students to develop their imaginative and intuitive capacity as well as fostering a curious and speculative disposition. Students apply these to propose novel ideas, develop original artefacts and make new connections.

The reasoning strand provides students with the knowledge and tools to both construct and evaluate ideas and arguments that may be unfamiliar. It underpins other areas of the curriculum in which students are required to gather, consider and evaluate data, evidence and propositions and then form conclusions.

The metacognition strand defines the knowledge and skills that enable students to better identify, describe, understand, practise, develop and manage their own learning processes. Critical and creative thinking processes are not discrete but are related within each of the strands.[11]

Second, rather than imposing the new capability on schools, it has been working with the Centre for Real-World Learning to prototype effective approaches to pedagogy. One of our earlier case studies, Brunswick East Primary School, is part of this group.

Third, Victoria's politicians have decided that capabilities, like disciplinary knowledge, will be assessed and have chosen initially to focus on critical and creative thinking. There is more on this in the next chapter.

Key learning points

VCAA's highlighting of critical and creative thinking is reflected in the key learning points:

1. Keep the description of critical and creative thinking as simple as possible.
2. Consider progression over two years rather than one.
3. Invest in professional learning for teachers and school leaders.

---

[11] For more on the Victorian curriculum see: http://victoriancurriculum.vcaa.vic.edu.au/critical-and-creative-thinking/introduction/learning-in-critical-and-creative-thinking.

4. Develop bottom-up solutions and share promising practices.

5. Use assessment to drive change.

6. Connect policy, research and practices.

New Pedagogies for Deeper Learning, Canada – research based, clarity of progression within its defined capabilities and a commitment to pedagogies for building capabilities

Initially developed by Michael Fullan in Toronto, Canada, and colleagues Greg Butler, Joanne McEachen and Joanne Quinn, New Pedagogies for Deeper Learning (NPDL) has become a global movement, currently active in seven countries, offering support to schools to develop the kinds of capabilities young people need today. It focuses on 6 Cs:

1. Creativity: Having an 'entrepreneurial eye' for economic and social opportunities, asking the right enquiry questions to generate novel ideas, and leadership to pursue those ideas and turn them into action.

2. Critical thinking: Critically evaluating information and arguments, seeing patterns and connections, constructing meaningful knowledge and applying it in the real world.

3. Collaboration: Working interdependently and synergistically in teams with strong interpersonal and team-related skills, including effective management of team dynamics and challenges, making substantive decisions together, and learning from and contributing to the learning of others.

4. Citizenship: Thinking like global citizens, considering global issues based on a deep understanding of diverse values and worldviews, and with a genuine interest and ability to solve ambiguous and complex real-world problems that impact human and environmental sustainability.

5. Character: Learning to 'deep learn', armed with the essential character traits of grit, tenacity, perseverance and resilience, and the ability to make learning an integral part of living.

6. Communication: Communicating effectively using a variety of styles, modes and tools (including digital tools), tailored for a range of audiences.

For each of the 6 Cs there is a detailed road map describing the journey towards proficiency.

There is considerable overlap with our model of creative thinking and much synergy between the kinds of pedagogies proposed by NPDL and those suggested in this book. The deep learning in NPDL's title is created by using precisely the kinds of signature pedagogies we describe in Chapters 2 and 3.

Central to NPDL's approach is the creation of networks of five or more schools, as well as clusters of more than a hundred, often with a relationship with a state or country. Networks and clusters all commit to use a collaborative enquiry process where students design, assess and monitor their own learning; teachers collaborate to assess, design, implement, reflect and adjust learning; and leaders assess the learning conditions that support deep learning and design strategies to create improved conditions.

Key learning points

The key learning points emerging from NPDL's work include:

1. Make a focus on capabilities part of a global campaign.
2. Invest in professional learning.
3. Organise in professional learning communities.
4. Specify progression within capabilities.

Four Dimensional Education, USA – research based, clarity of progression within its defined competencies and an alliance of education leaders

Four Dimensional Education (4DE) is the approach to education advocated by the Partnership for 21st Century Learning (P21). As well as subject knowledge, 4DE advocates four competencies or learning and innovation skills. Its 4 Cs are creativity, critical thinking, communication and collaboration. 4DE separates creativity from critical thinking, taking its definition of creativity from Jonathan Plucker and colleagues (2004, p. 90): 'Creativity is the interaction among aptitude, process, and environment by which an individual or group produces a perceptible product that is both novel and useful as defined within a social context.'

But, rather than limiting the focus to any one definition, 4DE offers a number of other well-evidenced frameworks and models on which practitioners can base their views. Critical thinking is also broadly scoped with many models and approaches offered: 'Reflective, analytical, evaluative, and deliberative skills and characteristics are common themes across these definitions, conceptualisations, and theories' (Dilley et al., 2015, p. 3).

Throughout this book, we have deliberately brought critical thinking and creativity together in our five-dimensional model of creative thinking rather than seeing them as separate capabilities. One of many helpful suggestions made by P21 is the idea that the cultivation of the 4 Cs need not just be confined to the classroom but extended across the whole system, as the table below suggests.

Cultivation of creative thinking: implications for practice

Level	Intervention	Assessment
Classroom	Make classroom settings more inviting for creative input and thinking; embed creativity within the classroom culture	Promote and incorporate student creativity outcomes in curriculum and instruction

Level	Intervention	Assessment
School	Embed creativity within the underlying culture of the school and make sure learning spaces support creative output	Develop a common vision, plan and strategy for incorporating creativity into teaching and learning; build staff capacity and support innovative teaching practices that develop creativity
Out of school	Evaluate the extent to which programmes, activities, services, spaces and culture support creativity; redesign learning/activity environment as needed	Incorporate creativity into programmes, activities and support services; support building staff capacity through professional development etc.
Local district	Determine how resources are used to promote creativity, boosting learning spaces and learning culture; allocate resources as needed	Provide professional development and resources to schools regarding creativity intervention practices
State	Support the incorporation of teaching practices and learning environments that promote creativity	Develop or make available professional development and curriculum that build capacity for incorporating creativity into teaching and learning
National	Devote resources to support creativity research, interventions and assessments	Fund development, pilot implementation and evaluation of creativity interventions

Source: Adapted from Plucker et al. (2015, p. 8)

Intervention, in the sense that it is used, includes pedagogy as we have applied it, but it is broader, also encompassing strategy. Assessment is used differently from our use of it here, moving out into system change. 4DE has a strong foundation of support in the United States and growing connections to thinkers across the world.

Key learning points

4DE's approach to creative thinking is reflected in these key learning points:

1. Link research, practice and policy.
2. Build alliances.
3. Exemplify promising practices.
4. Recognise that disciplinary, interdisciplinary and wider so-called twenty-first century competencies are all important.

Creative Schools

In terms of public interest and policy influence, Sir Ken Robinson has been a towering figure – initially leading an investigation into the role of arts in schools, then chairing an influential commission into the role of creativity in schools (Robinson, 1999) and latterly speaking via TED talks on stages across the world and through his many books.

More recently, in answer to the question, 'What's worth knowing?' he has defined creative schools in terms of eight core competencies (Robinson and Aronica, 2015):

1. Curiosity: The ability to ask questions and to explore how the world works.
2. Creativity: The ability to generate new ideas and to apply them in practice.

3. Criticism: The ability to analyse information and ideas to form reasoned arguments and judgements.

4. Communication: The ability to express thoughts and feelings clearly in a range of media and forms.

5. Collaboration: The ability to work constructively with others.

6. Compassion: The ability to empathise with others and to act accordingly.

7. Composure: The ability to connect with the inner life of feeling and develop a sense of personal harmony and balance.

8. Citizenship: The ability to engage constructively with society and to participate in the processes that sustain it.

These competencies, we would say capabilities – especially curiosity, creativity, criticism, communication and collaboration – align closely with the arguments we make in this book.

Key learning points

The key learning points from Sir Ken Robinson's work on creativity in schools include:

1. Inspire in person.

2. Use the web to inspire at scale.

3. Use research, story, anecdote and argument.

4. Appeal to the grass roots.

Educating Ruby and Building Learning Power, UK

At exactly the same time as Sir Ken Robinson and Lou Aronica brought out their book, *Creative Schools*, Guy Claxton and Bill Lucas published *Educating Ruby: What Our Children Really Need to Learn* (2015). More than a book, this is a change project seeking to talk directly to parents, and bringing together thought leaders, influential organisations and many schools to think systematically about how to change the way schools are organised. The ideas in *Educating Ruby* draw on Guy's Building Learning Power, a framework now in use in thousands of schools across the world, on the concept of Expansive Education (co-developed with Ellen Spencer) and on collaborative thinking and writing at the Centre for Real-World Learning.

Ruby has 7 Cs – confidence, curiosity, collaboration, communication, creativity, commitment and craftsmanship. These are both similar to and different from the other capabilities or competencies proposed in this chapter. We imagine what Ruby, the fictional granddaughter of the fictional Rita (in the film and play *Educating Rita* by Willy Russell) might say if she bumped into the head teacher of her school once she has left. We over-egg the dialogue somewhat just to make a point (here in a slightly edited version)!

> You helped me develop my *confidence*. By the way your teachers responded to me, you gave me faith that what I thought was worth thinking. You gave me the feeling that there were many worthwhile things I could achieve and become, if I put my mind to it, even though they were not academic things. And you made me discover that, if I put in the effort, it often paid off. By pushing me and not giving up on me, you helped me learn to be a can-do sort of person.
>
> You helped me become *curious*. When I asked questions your teachers didn't make me feel stupid or tell me 'I should have been listening'. If my questions were off-piste you explained why in a respectful way. You encouraged us all to try new things, and made it so nobody ever laughed at anyone for having a go, even if they weren't very good to start with. I learned that everyone makes mistakes: it doesn't mean you are no good, it means you are learning. So I'm always up for a challenge now, and I'm exploring all kinds of things I would never have dreamed of.
>
> You helped us all become convivial, *collaborative* kinds of people. Your teachers showed us how to discuss and disagree respectfully, so we naturally treated each other like that. You taught us never to laugh at someone for not knowing things. You helped us understand why it is so important for our own sake to be trustworthy

and honest in our dealings with people – and to admit when we had screwed up or apologise when we said something out of order.

You definitely helped me become more *communicative*. Because I learned to enjoy reading, I think I have a better understanding of people and a richer vocabulary – especially for talking about emotional or intimate kinds of things. We talked a lot in class, and your teachers helped us recognise the different kinds of talk we could have, and how to be appropriate. And I learned that sometimes I need to be quiet and by myself, too, and that doesn't mean I'm shy or upset. I've learned that sometimes I need to stop and think before I speak – but not always.

You helped me discover my own *creativity*. Your teachers often set us puzzles and asked us for our ideas, so we got used to thinking aloud and building on what other people had said. We learned not to dismiss things that sounded daft too quickly, because they could often lead to interesting and novel ideas. Some teachers even taught us how to do whacky things, like learn to toggle between being clear and logical and then going dreamy and imaginative – how to control our own minds better to get the most out of them.

You helped us all discover the value of being *committed* to what we do. Through being given the chance to learn independently, you helped me learn to take responsibility, to sort things out for myself, and to stick with hard things and not wait to be rescued. I'm not afraid of hard work, and you showed me that worthwhile things usually don't come easily, so when I do go to university (I will, you know) I will be ready for the self-discipline and slog I will need to put in.

And you also taught me the pleasures of *craftsmanship*. I used to be a bit slap-dash, but now I take a real pride in producing work that is as good as I can make it. I don't want to let the others down, but more importantly I don't want to let myself down. It's not just about determination; it's about being careful, thinking about what you are doing, taking time to reflect and improve, going over your mistakes and practising the hard parts.

Key learning points

The key learning points to emerge from *Educating Ruby* include:

1. Appeal to parents directly.
2. Show how we need both subject knowledge *and* capabilities.
3. Show how it can be done despite the system in many countries.
4. Redefine character education.

In this chapter we've seen, most importantly, how a small number of schools across the world are blazing a trail with regard to creative thinking (these schools are just the tip of the iceberg). But perhaps, most interestingly, we have laid out an impressive coalition of academics, policy-makers and governments who are beginning to describe the frameworks within which many more schools can flourish as they, too, embed creative thinking in their disciplinary curriculum life as well as their co-curricular activities, which can, in turn, support practices in their local, regional and national systems.

Chapter 6
Signs of Success

Some suggestions as to how student progress can be assessed

> Turning finally to the wider context for assessing and recording creativity, there is a case for examining the relationship between fostering creativity and the bureaucratic arrangements for the quality assurance of teaching and learning, including subject-centred level grading of achievements of both teachers and pupils.
>
> Anna Craft, *An Analysis of Research and Literature on Creativity in Education* (2001, p. 24)

Most schools do not assess creative thinking. They don't do it for a number of reasons. In the main, national assessments measure disciplinary or subject knowledge or skills of some kind, so teachers focus on these rather than on capabilities. Some teachers are worried that assessing creative thinking is a bit too close to assessing personality or possibly that it will be overly reductive, ending up with, say, a 'level 4b in creative thinking'. Many simply do not know how to go about assessing progress in creative thinking in already very demanding jobs. And, as the quotation from Anna Craft above implies, the gravitational pull of subjects is so great that it dominates thinking about what success is, both for pupils and teachers.

But across the world there is growing evidence that creative thinking should and can be assessed. It should be assessed primarily because assessment is vital for any learner to be able to monitor their progress; used formatively, assessment helps pupils to make better progress. The process of assessing requires us to think fundamentally about the essence of what we are assessing — the five habits and their sub-habits in our model. This helps teachers and students to be clearer about what *it* is and understand *it* more. Pragmatically speaking, if creative thinking is assessed it is likely to be easier for teachers to prioritise its inclusion in busy schools.

The evidence is growing that creative thinking can be assessed. In the last chapter, we shared the OECD and state of Victoria examples and showed how two secondary schools in England and Australia have promising practices to share. But measuring the development of capabilities such as creative thinking requires teachers to adapt some techniques with which they are already familiar and develop some new ones.

In this chapter, we offer some suggestions as to what you could try in your school if you find the idea of assessing creative thinking a helpful one. We have deliberately used the phrase 'tracking progress' rather than 'assessment' to encourage those who might otherwise see assessment of creative thinking as undesirable. It also makes it more likely that the activity will be seen as a formative process actively involving learners.

The table below shows some of the different approaches being used by schools and in this chapter we highlight some examples which may be useful.

Approaches to assessing capabilities

Pupil	**Teacher**	**Real-world**	**Online**
Real-time feedback	Criterion-referenced grading	Expert reviews	Reliable, validated online tests
Photos	Structured interviews	Gallery critique	Digital badges
Self-report questionnaires	Rating of products and processes	Authentic tests, e.g. displays, presentations, interviews, podcasts, films	E-portfolios
Logs/diaries/journals	Performance tasks		
Peer review	Capstone projects	Exhibitions	
Group critique			
Badges			
Portfolios			

Before we look at each of these four approaches in more detail, it may be helpful to establish some ground rules or principles for the assessment of capabilities. (The first three are similar to any assessment and the last two of particular relevance to creative thinking.)

1. It needs to be reliable. If you weigh a bag of apples at different times of day and in different rooms, you want the scales to record the same weight. The same is true for assessing, let's say, inquisitiveness (although it is rather more complex!).

2. It needs to be valid. That is to say, it needs to measure what it sets out to measure. In our context it needs to be, say, tracking progress in inquisitiveness rather than collaboration.

3. It needs to be timely. It's going to be most helpful if pupils get feedback as they are learning so they can act upon it.

4. It needs to draw on more than one source of evidence. If you are trying to measure an individual's ability to be persistent, for example, you might like to hear a learner's perspective, have a teacher's observation of persistence in action and, perhaps, several drafts of an essay to act as evidence. This approach is often referred to as triangulation.

5. It needs to be manageable. Whatever you decide upon, it needs to pass your common sense test that it is actually doable alongside your other demands. The best way of making any assessment manageable is to integrate it into teaching and learning so that it happens all the time rather than as an add-on.

Pupils tracking progress

Once upon a time pupils were assessed and not assessors. But this is no longer the case, largely as the result of the evidence produced by the AfL movement which has shown how formative assessment improves outcomes. Dylan Wiliam (2006, p. 6) argues that there are five core strategies in AfL:

1. Clarifying and understanding learning intentions and criteria for success.
2. Engineering effective classroom discussions, questions and tasks that elicit evidence of learning.
3. Providing feedback that moves learners forward.
4. Activating students as instructional resources for each other.
5. Activating students as owners of their own learning.

These five strategies will inform interactions with pupils. In terms of more specific ways in which pupils can engage, here are some suggestions.

Real-time feedback

Pupils could spend a few minutes at the end of a class looking over each other's work and sharing something they liked and something which could be 'even better if'. Pupils can be given a role such as 'question monitor' or 'persistence checker' during a lesson and then encouraged to give quick verbal feedback at the end of a lesson, commenting on pupils who have demonstrated these habits. Many AfL techniques, such as traffic lights (red – don't understand, not confident; amber – beginning to grasp this, getting there; green – totally get it, feeling confident) can be applied to aspects of creative thinking.

Photos

Many schools have 'bring your own device' policies which actively encourage students to use their mobile devices. In this case, it is an easy matter for pupils to scan examples of their work and upload to a secure area (see also 'Portfolios', page 167, and 'E-portfolios', page 178).

Self-report questionnaires

A self-report questionnaire is a series of statements or questions which pupils use to self-rate. Typically they might be framed as can-do statements or pupils might be given alternative words to choose such as 'never', 'sometimes', 'often', 'always' to describe the degree to which they are confident in a course of action, or 'not at all', 'quite', 'very', 'extremely' to describe their degree of confidence with regard to a particular activity. Another way of developing these is to produce a statement such as, 'I always keep going when I get stuck', and ask the children to say whether it is 'like me' or 'not like me'. If this is represented graphically it is possible to create a sliding scale to enable pupils to show their progress.

Self-reports like these can be a useful tool in helping pupils to start to use and understand language to describe their progress. On their own they are neither valid nor reliable, but set against other measures, such as teachers' observations, they can be very useful.

Thomas Tallis School uses a four-stage process to track student progress in each of our fifteen sub-habits: beginning–developing–confident–expert. They have also adapted our work to represent the progress graphically rather than in statements. A copy of their assessment wheel appears on page 164, and a full-colour expanded model appears on the inside back cover.

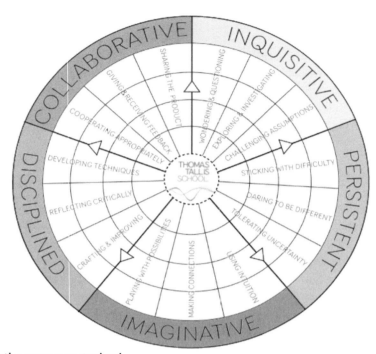

How to use the assessment wheel

Shade the segment of the circle that best represents how confident you feel about possessing each Habit of Mind. The levels of confidence grow in strength outwards from the centre of the wheel.

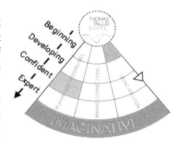

For example, as far as being imaginative is concerned, you may feel like your ability to use your intuition is just beginning whereas you are more confident in playing with possibilities. Be honest, reflect carefully and try to think of specific examples of each ability before you identify your level of confidence.

The creative habits of mind assessment wheel

Logs/diaries/journals

Making time to reflect is a good thing in its own right. Reflections can be as simple as a short sentence about progress in a class, done routinely, or more extended pieces of reflective writing. A really simple way of structuring end-of-session reflections on progress is to pre-format slips of paper, developing an idea from Edward de Bono.

A structured reflection tool

Plus	Minus	Interesting
Something that went well today was …	Something that did not go so well today was …	Something that surprised me today was …

Peer review

Peer review is much used in higher education where students might be asked to review each other's draft papers. It is also very effective when teachers visit each other's schools as peer reviewers to observe colleagues in action. But it can also work well in a class where its focus is on an aspect of creative thinking. Let's suppose you were looking at 'crafting and improving'. Pupils might work together in pairs to look at the ways in which, over a series of lessons, each had been crafting and improving, for example, a presentation about the local history of their area and why it would be of interest to a foreign visitor. You'd need to give some guidance – possibly some templates – to the pupil reviewers. This might be:

1. Start with something you liked and why.

2. Suggest one area for improvement using the words, 'You might like to …' (see Sub-habit 8 in Chapter 3).

3. End with something like, 'How does that seem to you?'

Group critique

In Chapter 3 we introduced you to the idea of gallery critique (see Sub-habit 8), but there are many kinds of structured ways in which pupils can be coached to give and receive feedback from each other (a core aspect of creative thinking and, indeed, of learning more generally). Routinely sharing one another's work-in-progress and critiquing it is a key studio habit according to Lois Hetland (Hetland et al., 2007). That is to say, it is something that anyone making anything needs to grasp and see as valuable. All pupils should learn to think and talk with others about aspects of their work (or work-in-progress) and develop confidence and skill in evaluating the work of others. Increasingly, it is helpful if students are aware of what progression looks like within creative thinking.

Badges

For many decades, organisations like the scouts and guides have rewarded achievement, typically in skills, by giving activity badges which would then be sewn onto a child's uniform. These might be for things like hiking, map-reading, volunteering, cooking, caring for an animal, survival skills and so on. While these are more activity based, some badges are closer to aspects of creative thinking such as 'Communicator' or 'Personal Challenge'. Organisations like the Royal Yachting Association, which teaches young people to sail, are also explicitly recognising capabilities which make up creative thinking. The parenting organisation MarvellousMe has created an app of the same name that contains a set of badges which recognise progress in creative thinking.[1] Badges can be sent electronically by teachers to parents to reward their children's achievements. It is a relatively

---

1 See https://marvellousme.com/.

small step from here for schools to create their own badges for the five dimensions or sub-dimensions of creative thinking. Many are already doing so, as a quick web search will show you. Digitisation has allowed badges to take a huge step forward in two areas: they can be customised to suit any area and they can include digital forms of proof of learner progress (see 'Digital badges' on page 177).

Portfolios

Portfolios have a long history in art, design, architecture and creative writing. They are a good way of encouraging learners to select their best work. They also enable learners to show how they have developed and progressed through different drafts, developing their capabilities in being both persistent and disciplined. They are a really good way of charting the development of creative thinking. Just stop and ask yourself what evidence you might want to see to show that a student has made progress in any one of the fifteen sub-habits of creative thinking and you have in effect begun to imagine what a portfolio might look like. Increasingly these will be digital (see 'E-portfolios' on page 178).

Teachers tracking progress

Criterion-referenced grading

Teachers will be only too familiar with the concept of progression within a subject, where pupils are graded according to the level of achievement. But the fundamental difference here is that, while knowledge and skill will clearly be part of an overall assessment, we are fundamentally looking at capability. 'Wondering and questioning' is not the same as times tables. 'Daring to be different' is different from knowing the causes of the First World War. 'Playing with possibilities' is a fair stretch away from accurately translating Spanish into English.

A number of organisations and a few countries and states across the world have begun to undertake the process of mapping progression in creative thinking. Each uses a slightly different definition of creative thinking but the principle is clear. Australia has mapped progression by year for critical and creative thinking. The state of Victoria has chosen to simplify this and assume that progress in capability growth might better be charted over two-year periods, given that it may not be quite as age related as in, say, mathematics. The example below is taken from one of our case studies in Chapter 5 (New Pedagogies for Deeper Learning). It seeks to describe progress at different levels.

Of course, this is not straightforward. Context matters. It's not easy to fairly represent development in something like 'daring to be different', where it is only the observable behaviour and not the internal struggle that can be judged. Progress does not happen evenly and can, as the teenage years arrive, even regress! But provided that this kind of teacher observation is combined with other sources of data, then it is likely that assessment will be more reliable.

As with any kind of teacher-observed assessment using criteria, it will be important for teachers to meet and go through a moderation process. This has various benefits: it improves teacher understanding of the topic of creative thinking, it enables them to share practices and, most importantly, it improves the quality of assessments.

New Pedagogies for Deeper Learning – Creativity

Having an entrepreneurial eye for economic and social opportunities, asking the right enquiry questions to generate novel ideas, and leadership to pursue those ideas and turn them into action.

Limited evidence

- Learners are unable to spot opportunities to create value or meet social or economic needs.

- Learners engage in the topic but struggle to generate significant questions to inspire deep exploration of real-world issues or problems.

- Learners look for predetermined solutions.

- Learners cannot lead a vision to reality.

- Learners are unlikely to have the skills or confidence to bring others together to realise their vision.

Emerging

- With guidance, learners begin to develop an entrepreneurial way of looking for needs, problems or opportunities to solve for economic and/or social benefit.

- With guidance, learners are beginning to generate enquiry questions to identify need/opportunities.

- Learners have a limited range of thinking and creativity strategies to find genuine value-added innovations.

- Learners can lead parts of tasks/experiences but not to completion.

Developing

- Learners are able to find opportunities to solve real problems that deliver social/economic benefit.

- Learners can identify real-world issues and problems and can pose good enquiry questions for authentic purposes.

- Learners are starting to diverge/move out of their comfort zones to think in different ways to identify and evaluate promising ideas.

- Learners are developing skills in creative thinking strategies. They demonstrate action-orientated leadership (i.e. decisions, roles) and can see the vision.

- Learners are developing good action-oriented leadership skills and decision-making to form balanced teams, build a vision of success and the steps to make it happen.

Accelerating

- Learners have a strong entrepreneurial drive (risk-taking, vision, motivation, etc.) to find solutions that are economically and socially viable and can mobilise talents/teams to fulfil needs or create opportunities.

- Learners have well-established enquiry skills, can identify risks and challenges, generate essential questions, provocations and wonderings, and can design an enquiry process to understand the issue in its real-world context.

- Learners exhibit good divergent thinking and are skilled at a wide range of creative thinking strategies.

- Learners actively pursue ideas that are innovative or risky to ensure solutions add value. They have strong action leadership skills and a can-do attitude. They leverage expertise and resources to achieve desired outcomes.

- Learners have strong leadership for action skills, organising clear paths for progress, utilising strengths and building skills and knowledge.

> ## Proficient
>
> - Learners have a talent for identifying opportunities with social, environmental or economic value.
>
> - Learners are skilled at framing problems and posing questions, actively grappling with big ideas, challenging the status quo and exhibiting genuine curiosity.
>
> - Learners have an eye for novel ideas, can integrate multiple perspectives and can pursue these to fruition.
>
> - Learners display leadership skills and can bring people with them to create deep change for exciting/inspiring others.
>
> - Learners have the perseverance and vision to lead a task to a promising outcome.

Teacher-observed assessment criteria for creativity

Source: Adapted from NPDL

Structured interviews

In working life or in research, much is learned about the quality of processes and of thinking through structured interviews in which the same questions are asked to different individuals, allowing the asker to explore the full extent of variation. Simply by posing the creative thinking habits as questions with pupils, you can begin to see how questions could be framed which would be useful both formatively and summatively.

Rating of products and processes

Teachers can set assignments that require students to design/plan and construct/compose a product, demonstrating their understanding of certain knowledge and application of skills. A 'product' might be a piece of written work, like a book review, poem or research report. It might involve design – an advert, experiment or floor plan. It could involve composition of music, photography or drawing. Students would have sight of clear assessment criteria, and rating could be carried out by teachers, peers, 'experts', students themselves or a combination.

Performance tasks

The two main performance tasks in tests of knowledge and skill are essays and answering pre-set questions, whether as multiple-choice, an opportunity for producing free text or numeric questions, perhaps showing your workings as you do so. These are hardly appropriate for creative thinking. Performance tasks here might include many of the examples in the next section on real-world assessment such as presentations, interviews, debates, role plays, podcasts and films.

Capstone projects

These are more long-term investigative projects where students attempt to apply curriculum learning to a specific idea. As such, they tend to take place at the end of an academic programme. Findings may be presented in various ways, including a final product, portfolio, performance, paper or presentation. These projects can provide an opportunity for interdisciplinary critical thinking, and allow students to bring in out-of-school experiences to connect to community issues, for example.

Real-world assessment options

Real-world and online assessment options are, arguably, the ones where most innovation is now taking place. Although we have been focusing on the role of teachers in developing creative thinking, the concept is much bigger than school. It is a capability for the real world of home, community and work as well as education, and, as such, can benefit from the input of many beyond school. Real-world assessment begins with the end in mind, thinking back from the desired real-life attribute to the kinds of assessment which would most accurately tell you that the goal had been accomplished.

If you wanted to create engineers, for example, taking a paper-and-pencil maths or science test of is far less relevance than having to go through the engineering design process (see the figure on on page 38), struggle with a genuine problem in small groups using high level applied maths and science techniques, and present your findings to actual engineers working locally. Real-world assessment techniques help us to see the difference between knowing something or being able to do something and actually applying knowledge or actually doing things skilfully in context.

Expert reviews

Think of all the subjects you currently teach and then consider who in the school community might be an expert. The engineering example above is a relatively obvious one. But what about people who use English for a living — journalists, publishers, editors, poets, song-writers. Or maths — accountants, designers, small business owners. Or science — ecologists, doctors, nurses, vets, pharmacists, engineers. Or art and design — actors, musicians, painters, sculptors, gallery curators, web designers. Humanities — archaeologists, town planners, travel agents, museum workers. The list is endless. Now make a mental connection between potential experts, possibly parents or local people, and the dimensions of creative thinking and imagine who might be the best individuals to act as expert assessors. Added advantage of engaging with such people is the likelihood that their enthusiasm will rub off on students, who will also be able to make the connection between their work in class and future possible careers.

Now read on to consider some of the ways in which experts could play a part.

Gallery critique

We have already met this technique in terms of student-to-student feedback. All that needs to be done to extend this out from school is to locate it in a community space, either on the school site or in a neutral venue, such as a local library or community hall, where community members can offer feedback to students in both written form (on sticky notes, electronically) or in person (students can be present at certain known times).

Authentic tests

Displays, presentations, interviews, podcasts and films may already be part of your school's approach to teaching, learning and assessment, or you may be swamped by the more traditional paper-and-pencil model of testing. They provide two kinds of opportunity: authenticity and a chance not just to create final 'products' but also to see into the thinking which lies behind a student's work.

Displays of work (or work-in-progress) are perhaps the easiest to organise as they can be viewed at times to suit outside experts. Presentations often form part of existing assessment practices but these can be developed to offer specific opportunities to show creative thinking. An example would be *Dragon's Den* type pitching of ideas to local business people. Or it could simply be a short slide show presentation to invited experts where the student has been asked to demonstrate specific knowledge, skill and capability.

Interviews are effective ways of seeing how a pupil is thinking about a topic and can work well both ways (i.e. student interviewing expert or expert interviewing student). Group interviews also provide opportunities to assess collaboration in practice. Podcasts, like talks, provide an additional opportunity to inject urgency (against a clock), authenticity (widely used on websites) and critical reflection (can be reviewed and learned from later). Other authentic assessment methods include: blogs (giving audience, context and length), web pages (requiring connection-making to other aspects of a site or the web), case studies (requiring deep understanding and the ability to investigate, challenging assumptions and developing techniques), learning logs (an obvious chance to develop critical reflection), field reports (requiring connection-making and collaboration), podcasts and radio broadcasts (like podcasts but increasingly schools have these set up; see the Our Lady of Victories case study in Chapter 5), posters and question banks (essential for anyone undertaking interviewing and an excellent way of developing and testing inquisitiveness) and wikis (a medium of our day, the design of which requires many of the dimensions of creative thinking and encourages students to follow their passions).

Exhibitions

It is a tenet of problem-based learning that exhibitions provide useful structure and motivation to students, especially when they know at the outset of a piece of investigation that there is a time and date set for the exhibition of their work. They offer a good opportunity to move into the real world by choosing a library, museum, gallery, outside space, cafe or church as a location. While exhibitions are like the various approaches listed above, they are different too in that, where they work best, students are actively involved in their planning. Indeed, the teacher should be much more of an observer than a participant or organiser. A really good resource exploring the logistics in more detail is Alec Patton's *Work That Matters* (2012), which is based on a collaboration with High Tech High in the United States.

Online assessment options

It was, arguably, PISA's 2015 decision to test collaborative problem-solving largely online that paved the way for this mode of assessment to become much more accepted, alongside, too, the growth of appropriate technologies.

Reliable, validated online tests

Just as teachers can use criteria to judge the standard of students' work, so, increasingly, computers can play a key role in assessing student progress. One particular benefit of the latest technology is that it can explore not just a student's answer to a question or puzzle, but all the choices that a learner makes along the way. This is particularly helpful when looking at creative thinking, a capability where there is frequently no one right answer to a question. The Victorian Curriculum and Assessment Authority (see the Brunswick East Primary School case study in Chapter 5) leads the world in developing online assignments which can provide reliable and valid snapshots of student progress. The approach they have adopted is to create a bank of simulations where, as in computer games, the subject matter is so intrinsically interesting that students are motivated to complete the tasks. They are true examples of assessment *as* learning. Here's an example of one of their prototypes:

Screenshot of an online assessment task

Source: Victorian Curriculum and Assessment Authority

Digital badges

Earlier, we explored the use of badges in providing validation of student achievement. A student who is a scout, for example, might develop persistence by visiting and caring for an elderly resident in a local care home over a period of time and be given a badge to recognise this achievement once she or he has met certain criteria. With advances in technology has come the opportunity to develop what are being called 'open badges' – that is to say, online badges which 'contain' evidence of a learner's capability.[2] Evidence can take many forms: photographs, work, testimonials, certificates and so on. An online badge is a kind of digital

---

2   See https://openbadges.org/.

'backpack' in which learners can keep examples of their work which demonstrate their capabilities.

These badges are a form of digital résumé or CV. As well as the obvious portability and transferability, an online badge has many other benefits. It directly involves the student in thinking about when they are ready for accreditation and what evidence they might select to evidence this. It can be customised to suit a specific desired outcome. Unlike the pre-made cloth badge of a scout's uniform, these can be created relatively quickly and easily on demand, so it would be possible to create an online creative thinker badge or, perhaps more helpfully, a set of badges for different aspects of thinking creatively.

E-portfolios

Like online badges, e-portfolios use the benefits of technology to extend an established idea. An e-portfolio is a kind of online folder which can be organised to facilitate a focus on any aspect of learning. It is a repository of experiences, achievements and examples of work in any format that can be stored digitally. Rooty Hill High School (see Chapter 5) has developed an innovative approach to assessing creative thinking using e-portfolios. It has created a digital learning hub on which each student has a space to record their progress. It is organised into the Australian capabilities, one of which is critical and creative thinking.

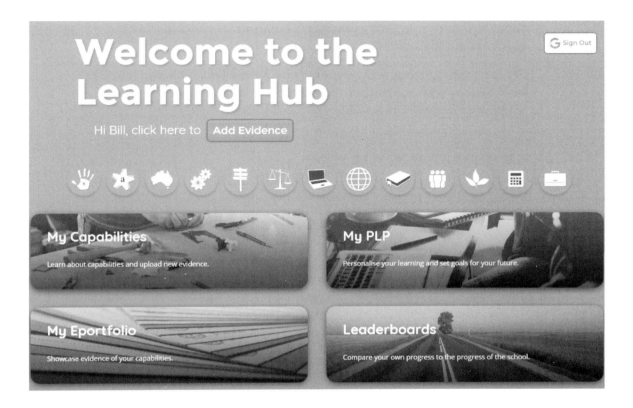

Screenshot of Rooty Hill's online creative thinking evidence repository

The learning hub enables students to:

- Find out more about each capability and upload evidence. This could be a document, video, audio recording or image. Evidence is validated (or not) by a teacher. Formal school assessments and externally validated certificates are automatically validated.

- Personalise their own learning and set goals. This section encourages students to describe challenges, pinpoint strategies and identify people who might help them. It invites students to reflect on their hobbies, extra-curricular interests, university aspirations (where appropriate), strengths, areas for development, additional responsibilities and career aspirations.

- Showcase evidence on their e-portfolio. This organises evidence into the different capabilities within the Australian curriculum.

- Compare their progress with other students in the school. This introduces a mildly competitive opportunity for students to see who is the 'top' student within specific capabilities, within a year and within a faculty.

Thomas Tallis School (see Chapter 5) has a similar approach to Rooty Hill and is developing an app to facilitate this process.

Chapter 7
Creative Challenges

Some pitfalls and how to avoid them

> [V]ery often, the movement for twenty-first century skills is a codeword for removing knowledge from the curriculum, and removing knowledge from the curriculum will ensure that pupils do not develop twenty-first century skills.
>
> Daisy Christodoulou, *Seven Myths About Education* (2013, p. 53)

> When I share these thoughts in public people always dismiss them as impractical. [They say] ... it's just not feasible. There's no time. Tests are the only feasible assessment system.
>
> Ron Berger, *An Ethic of Excellence* (2003, p. 102)

It will come as no surprise to readers of this book to discover that not everyone agrees with the arguments we are advancing. Thinking in advance about likely objections and the answers to them, as well as learning from the experiences of those who have blazed a trail, is a sensible thing to do.

An immediate problem is that words mean different things to different people! So, for Daisy Christodoulou, 'twenty-first century skills' becomes synonymous with a mistaken attempt to remove knowledge from education, and she understandably questions their validity as a consequence. We strongly distance ourselves from this idea. Knowledge is critically important. We want to see deeply knowledgeable and passionate teachers working with young people. We also want such teachers and students to go beyond the boundaries of their subject disciplines. And we need them to cultivate creative thinking capabilities through a range of subjects in the formal curriculum and via opportunities in the co-curriculum. Incidentally, we dislike the term 'twenty-first century skills' because it a lazy descriptor of capabilities to simply define them by a century rather than using a more accurate term such as dispositions or capabilities for lifelong learning.

We also hear the voices of busy, hard-working teachers with their real-world concerns about time and tests which ring in the ears of Ron Berger. We believe that it is possible to teach more expansively so that children excel at the tests of both the classroom and of life. But immediately impacting upon teachers are the constraints of their own school setting, and these in turn are influenced by the education system within which the school acts.

Teachers may come up against numerous potential barriers to their attempts to develop creative thinking in the classroom in the form of doubts such as the following.

We'd love to do this kind of thing but it's our first job to think about exam results

Accountability mandates have increased the pressure on teachers to ensure pupils meet externally imposed standards. When teachers perceive that preparation for tests is their most pressing pedagogical goal, opportunities for creative learning often narrow. Yet it shouldn't be the case that teaching for academic knowledge and for critical thinking are mutually exclusive. In fact, many of the sub-elements of creative thinking – such as better questioning, persistence, giving and receiving feedback and deliberate practice – are explicitly associated with improvements in student attainment.

Budgets won't stretch to teacher development on learning

One of the most – if not *the* most – pressing concerns for teachers is the school's budget. In the UK, schools face cuts due to a growth in pupil numbers, to changes in the way teacher pensions are organised and to the macro-economic outlook, which means that central government spending on public services is not keeping pace with inflation. In most parts of the world there are similar economic pressures. But to conflate general austerity with an inability to change the way a school organises its professional learning is not helpful. Not only can the same amount of time be used differently, but new models of professional learning, such as action research, can be deployed at very little cost.

The syllabus doesn't leave much room for you to think about tomorrow's capabilities

Whenever human beings are asked to change anything they will, understandably, point to a lack of money or time. Certainly, life is very busy in schools. But when teachers plan ahead or review schemes of work it is a relatively easy matter to look not just at knowledge and skills but also at capabilities or habits of mind.

Here's an example of mathematics reframed as a set of eight mathematical habits of mind by a mathematician interested in teaching both knowledge and capabilities (adapted from Cuoco et al., 1996):

- Pattern sniffers: Always on the lookout for patterns and the delight to be derived from finding hidden patterns and then using shortcuts from them in their daily lives.

- Experimenters: Performing experiments, playing with problems and performing thought experiments, allied to a healthy scepticism for experimental results.

- Describers: Able to play the maths language game – for example, giving precise descriptions of the steps in a process, inventing notation, convincing others, and writing out proofs, questions, opinions and more polished presentations.

- Tinkerers: Taking ideas apart and putting them back together again.

- Inventors: Always inventing things – rules for a game, algorithms for doing things, explanations of how things work or axioms for a mathematical structure.

- Visualisers: Being able to visualise things that are inherently visual, such as working out how many windows there are on the front of a house by imagining them or using visualisation to solve more theoretical tasks.

- Conjecturers: Making plausible conjectures, initially using data and increasingly using more experimental evidence.

- Guessers: Using guessing as a research strategy, starting with a possible solution to a problem and working backward to achieve the answer.

This teacher could apply an equally clear subject-specific interpretation of our fifteen creative thinking sub-habits. In fact, any subject teacher could do this for their own subject (and in many cases find others who have done it beforehand[1]). Yes, this will take a little time, but it only needs to be done once. It is always difficult to do anything new if you are not prepared to invest a little time.

School inspectors won't be interested

Accountability bodies tend to approach issues such as creative thinking from the perspective of understanding how it may help to raise standards. While this is a legitimate question there are others that schools will want to ask, such as, does helping young people think creatively lead them to have more successful and more fulfilled lives? Ofsted recognises the relationship between creative thinking and achievement. Its report, *Learning: Creative Approaches That Raise Standards* (2010), echoes our question, commenting that approaches to teaching which encourage creative thinking 'had a perceptible and positive impact on pupils' personal development, and on their preparation for life beyond school' (ibid., p. 4). The report explored attempts by a number of schools to encourage pupils 'to be questioning, imaginative and open to possibilities, and to reflect critically on the effect of ideas and actions' (ibid., p. 4). These are clearly the sorts of creative thinking habits we believe are important, but are also ones Ofsted associate with 'standards'.

---

1   See the work of Art Costa and Bena Kallick, who have written extensively about this.

It's another one of those fads that will be forgotten when the pressure mounts

The idea of capabilities has been around for several decades. The ideas underpinning creative thinking have been around for more than fifty years. They are not going to go away! Certainly, if it's not valued in the same way as those things affected by external pressure are valued then, yes, a focus on creative thinking is likely to be difficult. But what if feedback about creative habits is built into whole-school assessment and all reporting, including that to parents? Both Thomas Tallis School and Rooty Hill High School's approaches do this. Schools which really embed their commitment to creative thinking recognise the long-term value of these approaches.

You're just talking about what good teachers do anyway

In a sense, yes. Good teachers know about and use pedagogy well. With practice they use it unconsciously and will adapt their approach to the needs in front of them. Our ten-dimensional framework shows the sorts of decisions (ten of them, at least!) that teachers are making *all the time* (see page 8). But we are talking about doing it deliberately: using a mix of five core pedagogies to develop creative thinking, specifically, in a way that is coherent. A good teacher will usually want to be reminded of these things and nudged back on track.

How do we ensure subject knowledge isn't downgraded? This sounds like progressive ideology

If you have read this far, you will be familiar with the false dichotomy debate between knowledge and skills; with the deceptive labelling of some approaches to teaching as 'progressive' and others as 'traditional'; with straw-man arguments that traditional education deems school as a task that must be endured and progressive education means the absence of rigour.

Head teacher and blogger Tom Sherrington (2014) recognises the distinction between the two 'supposedly opposing poles of traditional and progressive pedagogy'. Yet he suggests that both have a 'vital role' in the education of our children. He argues that 'for me, the important thing is that they are not inherently in opposition; they are intrinsically linked facets of excellent learning and an excellent education overall. They might even be considered to exist in a symbiotic relationship.'

The reality of classroom teaching is often that the 'best way' will depend at any given moment on the content being taught and the cohort doing the learning. Most teachers use an eclectic range of methods. By focusing on the needs of individuals, the average teacher is not trying to teach only what they feel is relevant to pupils' lives. Neither are they trying to promote relativism by utilising problem-based learning, projects or discovery learning. Projects and interdisciplinary teaching activities need not be the enemy of real, objective knowledge.

There are a number of myths in education. Daisy Christodoulou (quoted at the opening of this chapter) has suggested some which she observes. But the most damaging myth about our own type of approach to pedagogy is that a move to the left of our ten-dimensional framework – where capabilities are often (but not always) best learned – would require a downgrading of knowledge.

All students need powerful knowledge. Subject expertise is a key purpose of education because it helps us to understand the world around us. But how you teach that subject knowledge is what determines whether or not you foreground capabilities like creative thinking or focus more on recall to order.

I need to make sure students have mastered the facts

This is absolutely true irrespective of how content is taught. Maybe a teacher with this concern is thinking that if too much time is given to discovery learning, project-based learning or the jigsaw approach, for example, there will be no time to correct errors. But nothing about teaching creative thinking suggests that students are given permission to construct facts as they see fit and left uncorrected.

Let's take the jigsaw approach as an example. A teacher will need to find ways of ensuring that 'expert groups' research material in a sensible, critical way. This is a good opportunity to provide them with access to useful resources and guidance about the strengths/weaknesses of certain sources.

Teachers are well able to use their judgement to work out when it is important for pupils to get a thorough grounding in a skill or area of content before they start to use and apply it in more complex ways or adopt the kinds of pedagogical approaches described in this book.

Pupils don't respond well to being given less direction

Some probably won't, particularly if it is what they are used to. Weaning students used to wholly didactic approaches takes time, not that direct instruction is a bad thing. But if a student only receives their learning through direct instruction, how will they learn to challenge assumptions, be different and cooperate with others?

Teachers who use the simple rubric 'three before me' (see Chapter 3) rapidly see how quickly pupils can be proactive, less dependent and more resourceful in working out the answers to their own questions themselves.

We've got enough initiatives going on already in schools

Probably true. If you see teaching creative thinking as a bolt-on to the content, you'll see it as another hill to climb that you just don't have time for. But if you see the approaches that we and others in this book have articulated as a shift in education mindset that is enduring – not an initiative, not a project – then you may take a different view.

We have a high proportion of children who wouldn't 'get it'

Interestingly, while some teachers have in mind 'less able' pupils when they say this, others are thinking of the 'most able'! The challenge depends on what you think 'it' is. In the UK, the All-Party Parliamentary Group on Social Mobility (2012) challenged these ideas head on by arguing that those who are less able or come from the least disadvantaged contexts most need to develop skills in the areas of character and resilience.

Parents won't like it – they have high expectations

Parents do indeed want to know that their children are being well taught and will succeed in whatever public examinations are set in whatever country you are based. But they also want happy children and young men and women who, when they leave school, are employable. The CBI's First Steps campaign about the ways in which schools should be changing to develop capabilities as well as subject knowledge makes this point abundantly clear (CBI, 2012). It should help to reassure parents. Globally, the direction being taken by the OECD and its PISA tests should similarly help.

Do we do this all the time or can we teach it stand-alone?

Research shows that both explicit and embedded instructional approaches can develop thinking (Marin and Halpern, 2011). In making this point, the authors cite Robert Swartz's three principles for instructing students in critical thinking which are:

1. The more explicit teaching of thinking is, the greater impact it will have on students.

2. The more classroom instruction incorporates an atmosphere of thoughtfulness, the more likely students are to value good thinking.

3. The more the teaching of thinking is embedded into content instruction, the more students will give thought to what they are learning.

They summarise by suggesting that 'there is plentiful evidence to expect that together they are especially powerful' (ibid., p. 3).

In practice, schools may choose to introduce the ideas and concepts relating to critical and creative thinking explicitly, a little at a time. They would simultaneously focus on infusing habits into subject teaching. Rooty Hill, for example, has a holistic model but chooses to highlight certain aspects at any one time. Thomas Tallis adopts a similar approach, focusing on particular habits in different half terms. Redlands introduces methods and skills as they are required for new topics. Brunswick East teaches children thinking routines which they can apply in many contexts. Our Lady of Victories and Duloe suffuse the whole school with creativity.

Schools are pragmatic places, and while it may be desirable to make creative thinking an integral part of what they do, new year groups, new topics and new teachers can all be moments when a reminder or booster session may be helpful.

How do we fit this in?

There is no doubt that a standard school timetable limits opportunities for extended activities and deep investigation. It is not just that lessons are in short blocks scattered across the week, but overall teaching hours for any course limits what can be prioritised on the syllabus. And surely only a daring teacher would sacrifice shallow coverage of facts for time spent going deeper.

We started this chapter with Ron Berger reflecting on public perceptions to his ideas: 'people always dismiss them as impractical'. Just how he fits his extended projects into the school day may seem superhuman. Yet in one sense it is down to priorities. If we think examinations are the be-all and end-all, and are prepared to teach for shallow recall in a bid to get there, we will teach in one way. But why not do it slightly differently and develop pupils' ability to reflect critically or give feedback?

For our case study schools, various approaches are adopted. Fitting in extended periods of learning via themed weeks is popular. Where possible, schools might try what Our Lady of Victories does and create extended periods of learning.

We like Berger's advice (2003, p. 152) to those wanting to know where to begin. With the wisdom of experience, he says:

> Start small, I suggest. It is better to improve one aspect of a culture and do it really well than to take on too much too soon and do it poorly. Do something well and build from there. Find something that most people feel good about and willing to tackle, rather than having the idea imposed as a mandate from above.

As far as integrating capabilities into the curriculum, Australia is among the world leaders, and with international tests prioritising creative thinking, its star is rising. This important capability isn't yet a required aspect of the curriculum or a measured outcome of education in England. But we think it should be.

Appendix
An A–Z of Teaching and Learning Methods for Developing Creative Thinkers

To be creative, an idea must also be appropriate – useful and actionable.
Teresa Amabile, How to Kill Creativity (1998)

With starter activities for each of the fifteen sub-habits, as well as some more extended examples, there are four dozen to choose from in this book. In this short chapter we list them for ease of access. **Emboldened** activities are those which are described in more detail in Chapter 4.

Beginning at the end: Practising 'reverse engineering' of a story.

Brainstorming to suspend judgement: Developing tolerance for ambiguity by inviting ideas on a given topic and preventing premature closing down of lines of thought.

Bringing in an expert: Inviting people into the classroom who have experience in a particular field to show examples of their own work or introduce a topic with real-world anecdotes.

Cards for questions: Motivating pupils to ask 'good' questions using visual tokens that help the teacher keep track of who is asking the questions.

Children create their own philosophical questions: Developing communication and critical questioning by considering a key topic-related question in more depth.

Classic paper clip game: Using divergent thinking as pupils jot down as many uses for a paper clip as they can think of.

Co-create a visual reference of helpful phrases: Generating a useful phrase bank that pupils can refer to when commenting on one another's work.

Connections: Practising constructing connections between objects or concepts by working out which object/concept links a set of three others. Alternatively, finding creative ways of linking ten random objects.

Copying: Developing techniques by practising accurate copying.

Creating a rubric: Introducing some real-world standards to the assessment of a piece of 'authentic' work (perhaps by asking some local experts or parents) so the pupils know at the beginning of a topic what to aim for.

Critique work anonymously: Practising critique in a non-threatening way by using an anonymous piece of work and focusing on a narrow number of criteria.

Deliberate practice: Developing deliberate practice as you help pupils to break down a task into its constituent parts and think about how they might practise the parts they find most challenging.

Driving questions: Encouraging macro-level thinking by posing questions that link aspects of a unit of work or topic.

Exit tickets: Developing reflection (both teacher's and pupils') using an exit tickets format to elicit information about what pupils have/haven't understood or what worked/didn't work in the classroom.

Expansive questions: Reframing any fixed mindset thoughts about learners' intelligence by giving them sight of a bank of expansive questions.

Feedforward: Encouraging articulation of an individual's own learning struggles in a way that invites suggestions from peers.

'5 Whys' technique: Uncovering the root causes of a problem to stimulate thinking about imaginative solutions by probing each explanation with a further 'why?' question.

Good or bad: Examining deep-rooted assumptions by exploring the impact that different forms of technology/innovations have had on our lives.

Growth mindset prompts: Developing pupils' ability to stick with difficulty as they receive feedback on a piece of work, along with prompt cards that encourage them to reframe any fixed mindset thinking.

Guided gallery critique: Practising giving helpful feedback on others' work-in-progress.

'I wonder' questions: Encouraging students to wonder out loud by inviting them to share questions that demonstrate curiosity.

Jigsaw: Developing collaborative capabilities by using a jigsaw format that divides pupils into teams. It requires each member to become an expert in one aspect of the project for the purposes of teaching their team so that everyone can pass an end-of-topic assessment.

Learning logs: Encouraging critical reflection by providing space for learning logs that are added to briefly and at regular intervals.

List as many games as you can: Developing tolerance for uncertainty by asking pupils to make a list with minimal guidance and then reflecting on their decision-making as they choose what to include and what to leave out.

Mind mapping: Developing imagination with a mind mapping technique that pupils can draw on to organise key topics, content and ideas around a central concept.

Noticing everything: Developing pupils' ability to focus on a single thought, action or idea by guiding them to use their senses to observe something around them and think about what they notice.

Odd one out: Practising making connections between ideas within a topic – and expressing a rationale – by focusing on which object does not belong.

Playing with Belbin: Helping children understand the importance of team roles by looking at the characteristics of team members.

Predict future challenges: Developing tolerance for ambiguity by helping pupils predict what challenges might arise in their everyday lives and inviting suggestions for how they might act.

Question of the week: Helping everyone learn from good questions by making a note of the best questions pupils ask and encouraging class reflection on the question itself.

Reworking: Improving pupils' work by giving them the opportunity to address feedback on a piece of work or to reattempt a difficult question from last week's lesson.

Scaffolding: Developing self-reflection as you invite pupils to compare outcomes with intended outcomes and to think through how their learning can be applied to other situations.

Sequencing an assignment: Making connections between tasks that need doing by representing a larger task with a visual chart or other image that breaks it down.

Six Thinking Hats: Questioning from a range of perspectives – looking at the positives and the negatives, facts and feelings, creating possibilities and consolidating understanding – in order to consider all views in a given scenario.

Slow writing: Developing techniques in writing by directing pupils to write sentences to meet certain criteria, then to return to each sentence and consider each choice of word to see if an improvement can be made.

Socratic seminars: Developing inquisitiveness by using a Socratic seminar format that begins with a real-life question and values the process of checking understanding, supporting others' comments, building on others' reasoning and making a new argument.

'Stuck' poster: Developing persistence using Building Learning Power's 'stuck' poster to help focus pupils on useful techniques to try when they don't know what to do next.

Subject-related thinking hats: Practising using the Six Thinking Hats with reference to a broad subject-related theme.

Teacher prompts: Developing self-reflection by modelling what it looks like to self-talk through a problem in front of the class.

Team-building exercise: Developing relationships that will benefit collaborative work by using a fun team challenge.

Three before me: Developing resourcefulness by requiring pupils to search for answers in three places (including their peers) before asking for help from the teacher.

Visualise: Helping pupils reach a receptive state to absorb detail by visualising a passage read aloud and thinking about what might happen next.

Waiting time: Slowing down pupils' thinking to develop their intuition by requiring them to pause before responding to a question.

What do you think? Developing thinking routines by returning pupils' questions back to them, reframed as another question.

What does this remind you of? Helping pupils to make connections between a piece of text and themselves/other texts/the wider world by questioning to deepen their understanding of the text.

What makes you say that? Encouraging pupils to see multiple perspectives by asking them to think about their perceptions about a particular artefact and to explain their interpretations.

What might you need to know? Stimulating problem-finding by asking pupils to think about what they need to find out in order to complete a piece of work.

Wicked questions: Stimulating curiosity by inviting students to explore different levels of meaning through asking questions of a philosophical or values-driven orientation to reflect on meaning and significance.

We hope you find this A–Z list helpful. Perhaps you'd like to use it as a starting point for building a creative thinking resource list for your own school.

References

All-Party Parliamentary Group on Social Mobility (2012). *7 Key Truths about Social Mobility. Interim Report.* London: All-Party Parliamentary Group.

Amabile, T. (1998). How to Kill Creativity. *Harvard Business Review*, 76(5), 76–87. Available at: https://hbr.org/1998/09/how-to-kill-creativity.

Australian Curriculum, Assessment and Reporting Authority (ACARA) (2015). *General Capabilities in the Australian Curriculum.* Sydney: ACARA. Available at: http://v7-5.australiancurriculum.edu.au/GeneralCapabilities/Pdf/Overview.

Bacon, F. (1605). *Of the Proficience and Advancement of Learning, Divine and Human.* London: Parker, Son, and Bourn.

Beghetto, R. (2010). Creativity in the Classroom. In J. Kaufman and R. Sternberg (eds), *The Cambridge Handbook of Creativity.* Cambridge: Cambridge University Press, pp. 447–463.

Berger, R. (2003). *An Ethic of Excellence: Building a Culture of Craftsmanship with Students.* Portsmouth, NH: Heinemann.

Borgonovi, F. and Montt, G. (2012). Parental Involvement in Selected PISA Countries and Economies. OECD Education Working Paper no. 73. Paris: Organisation for Economic Co-operation and Development. Available at: http://www.oecd.org/officialdocuments/publicdisplaydocumentpdf/?cote=EDU/WKP(2012)10&docLanguage=En.

Buzan, T. and Buzan, B. (1993). *The Mind Map Book: How to Use Radiant Thinking to Maximize Your Brain's Untapped Potential.* New York: Plume.

Canny, B. (2016). Here Are the Skills You Will Need to Succeed and Earn Big Buckaroos, *FYA* (20 April). Available at: http://www.fya.org.au/2016/04/20/here-are-the-skills-you-will-need-to-succeed-and-earn-big-buckaroos/.

Carroll, L. (1872). *Through the Looking Glass, and What Alice Found There.* London: Macmillan and Co.

Catmull, E. (2008). How Pixar Fosters Collective Creativity. *Harvard Business Review*, 86(9), 64–72. Available at: https://hbr.org/2008/09/how-pixar-fosters-collective-creativity.

CBI (2012). *First Steps: A New Approach for Schools.* London: CBI. Available at: http://www.cbi.org.uk/insight-and-analysis/first-steps/.

Christodoulou, D. (2013). *Seven Myths About Education.* London: Curriculum Centre.

Claxton, G. (2002). *Building Learning Power.* Bristol: TLO Ltd.

Claxton, G. and Lucas, B. (2015). *Educating Ruby: What Our Children Really Need to Learn.* Carmarthen: Crown House Publishing.

Claxton, G., Lucas, B. and Webster, R. (2010). *Bodies of Knowledge: How the Learning Sciences Could Transform Practical and Vocational Education*. London: Edge Foundation.

Cloninger, K. (2006). Making Intuition Practical: A New Theoretical Framework for Education. *Curriculum and Teaching Dialogue*, 8(1/2), 15–28.

Coe, R., Aloisi, C., Higgins, S. and Elliot Major, L. (2014). *What Makes Great Teaching? Review of the Underpinning Research*. London: Sutton Trust. Available at: http://www.suttontrust.com/wp-content/uploads/2014/10/What-makes-great-teaching-FINAL-4.11.14.pdf.

Costa, A. and Kallick, B. (2000). Describing the Habits of Mind. In A. Costa and B. Kallick (eds), *Discovering and Exploring Habits of Mind*. Alexandria, VA: ASCD, pp. 21–40.

Craft, A. (2001a). *An Analysis of Research and Literature on Creativity in Education*. London: Qualifications and Curriculum Agency.

Craft, A. (2001b). Little c Creativity. In A. Craft, R. Jeffrey and M. Leibling (eds), *Creativity in Education*. London and New York: Continuum, pp. 45–61.

Craft, A. and Chappell, K. (2016). Possibility Thinking and Social Change in Primary Schools. *Education 3–13*, 44(4), 407–425. DOI: http://dx.doi.org/10.1080/03004279.2014.961947

Craft, A., Cremin, T., Burnard, P., Dragovic, T. and Chappell, K. (2013). Possibility Thinking: Cumulative Studies of an Evidence-Based Concept Driving Creativity. *Education 3–13*, 41(5), 538–556. DOI: http://dx.doi.org/10.1080/03004279.2012.656671

Crawford, M. (2015). *The World Beyond Your Head: How to Flourish in an Age of Distraction*. London: Penguin Random House.

Csikszentmihalyi, M. (1996). *Creativity: Flow and the Psychology of Discovery and Invention*. New York: HarperCollins.

Cuoco, A., Goldenberg, P. and Mark, J. (1996). Habits of Mind: An Organizing Principle for Mathematics Curricula. *Journal of Mathematical Behaviour*, 15(4), 375–402.

Davies, D., Jindal-Snape, D., Collier, C., Digby, R., Hay, P. and Howe, A. (2013). Creative Learning Environments in Education: A Systematic Literature Review. *Thinking Skills and Creativity*, 8, 80–91. DOI: http://dx.doi.org/10.1016/j.tsc.2012.07.004

de Bono, E. (1992). *Serious Creativity: Using the Power of Lateral Thinking to Create New Ideas*. London: HarperCollins.

de Bono, E. (1993). *Sur/petition: Going Beyond Competition*. London: HarperCollins.

Descartes, R. (1701). *Rules for the Direction of the Mind*. Amsterdam: P. and J. Blaeu.

Dewey, J. (1910). *How We Think*. Boston, MA: D. C. Heath and Co.

References

Didau, D. (2012). Slow Writing: How Slowing Down Can Improve Your Writing. *The Learning Spy* (12 May). Available at: http://www.learningspy.co.uk/english-gcse/how-to-improve-writing/.

Dilley, A., Kaufman, J. and Plucker, J. (2015). *What We Know About Critical Thinking*. Washington, DC: Partnership for 21st Century Learning.

Duckworth, A. (2016). *Grit: The Power of Passion and Perseverance*. London: Vermilion.

Duckworth, A., Peterson, C., Matthews, M. and Kelly, D. (2007). Grit: Perseverance and Passion for Long-Term Goals. *Journal of Personality and Social Psychology*, 92(6), 1087–1101. Available at: https://upenn.app.box.com/v/DuckworthPeterson.

Duckworth, A. and Seligman, M. (2005). Self-Discipline Outdoes IQ in Predicting Academic Performance of Adolescents. *Psychological Science*, 16(12), 939–944.

Dunn, D. (n.d.). Using Peer Assessment in the Primary Classroom. *Teach Primary*. Available at: http://www.teachprimary.com/learning_resources/view/using-peer-assessment-in-the-primary-classroom.

Duron, R., Limbach, B. and Waugh, W. (2006). Critical Thinking Framework for Any Discipline. *International Journal of Teaching and Learning in Higher Education*, 17(2), 160–166. Available at: http://www.isetl.org/ijtlhe/pdf/IJTLHE55.pdf.

Dweck, C. (2006). *Mindset: The New Psychology of Success*. New York: Ballantine Books.

Dyer, F. L. and Martin, T. C. (1910). *Edison: His Life and Inventions*, Volume 2. New York: Harper & Brothers.

Einstein, A. (2009 [1931]). *Einstein on Cosmic Religion and Other Opinions and Aphorisms*. Mineola, NY: Dover Publications.

Ericsson, K. A. (2016). *Peak: Secrets from the New Science of Expertise*. New York: Houghton Mifflin Harcourt.

Fawcett, D. (2012). Split Screen Teaching. *My Learning Journey* (19 April). Available at: http://reflectionsofmyteaching.blogspot.co.uk/2012/04/split-screen-teaching.html.

Fensham, P. A. and Marton, F. (1992). What Has Happened to Intuition in Science Education? *Research in Science Education*, 22(1), 114–122.

Friedman, T. (2005). *The World Is Flat: A Brief History of the 21st Century*. New York: Farrar, Straus and Giroux.

Gale, K. (2001). Teacher Education within Post-Compulsory Education and Training: A Call for a Creative Approach. In A. Craft, B. Jeffrey and M. Leibling (eds), *Creativity in Education*. London and New York: Continuum, pp. 103–115.

Gillies, R. (2006). Teachers' and Students' Verbal Behaviours During Cooperative and Small-Group Learning. *British Journal of Educational Psychology*, 76(2), 271–287. DOI: 10.1348/000709905X52337

Green, S. (2014). How Google Manages Talent [interview with Eric Schmidt and Jonathan Rosenberg]. *Harvard Business Review*. Available at: https://hbr.org/2014/09/how-google-manages-talent.

Guilford, J. P. (1950). Creativity. *American Psychologist*, 5(9), 444–454.

Gutman, L. and Schoon, I. (2013). *The Impact of Non-Cognitive Skills on Outcomes for Young People: Literature Review*. London: Institute of Education, University of London.

Harrington, D. M. (1990). The Ecology of Human Creativity: A Psychological Perspective. In M. A. Runco and R. S. Albert (eds), *Theories of Creativity*. Newbury Park, CA: SAGE Publications, pp. 143–169.

Hattie, J. (2009). *Visible Learning: A Synthesis of Over 800 Meta-Analyses Relating to Achievement*. Abingdon: Routledge.

Hattie, J. and Gan, M. (2011). Instruction Based on Feedback. In R. Mayer and P. Alexander (eds), *Handbook of Research on Learning and Instruction*. New York: Routledge, pp. 249–271.

Heckman, J. and Kautz, T. (2012). Hard Evidence on Soft Skills. *Labour Economics*, 19(4), 451–464.

Heckman, J. and Kautz, T. (2013). Fostering and Measuring Skills: Interventions That Improve Character and Cognition. NBER Working Paper no. 19656. New York: National Bureau of Economic Research.

Henriksen, D. and Mishra, P. (2013). Learning from Creative Teachers. *Creativity Now!* 70(5). Available at: http://www.ascd.org/publications/educational-leadership/feb13/vol70/num05/Learning-from-Creative-Teachers.aspx.

Hesse, F., Care, E., Buder, J., Sassenberg, K. and Griffin, P. (2015). A Framework for Teachable Collaborative Problem Solving Skills. In P. Griffin and E. Care (eds), *Assessment and Teaching of 21st Century Skills: Methods and Approach*. Dordrecht: Springer, pp. 37–56. DOI: 10.1007/978-94-017-9395-7_2

Hetland, L. E., Winner, E., Veenema, S. and Sheridan, K. M. (2007). *Studio Thinking: The Real Benefits of Visual Arts Education*. New York: Teachers' College Press.

International Baccalaureate Organization (2008). *IB Learner Profile Booklet*. Cardiff: International Baccalaureate Organization.

Judkins, R. (2015). *The Art of Creative Thinking*. London: Sceptre.

KEA (2009). *The Impact of Culture on Creativity: A Study Prepared for the European Commission (Directorate-General for Education and Culture)*. Brussels: European Commission.

Kolb, D. (1984). *Experiential Learning: Experience as the Source of Learning and Development*. Englewood Cliffs, NJ: Prentice-Hall.

Llinares, D. (2011). *The Astronaut: Cultural Mythology and Idealised Masculinity*. Newcastle upon Tyne: Cambridge Scholars Publishing.

Lucas, B., Claxton, G. and Spencer, E. (2013a). *Expansive Education: Teaching Learners for the Real World*. Maidenhead: Open University Press.

References

Lucas, B., Claxton, G., and Spencer, E. (2013b). Progression in Student Creativity in School: First Steps Towards New Forms of Formative Assessments. OECD Education Working Paper no. 85. DOI: http://dx.doi.org/10.1787/5k4dp59msdwk-en

Lucas, B., Hanson, J., Bianchi, L. and Chippindall, J. (2017). *Learning to Be an Engineer: Implications for the Education System – Summary Report*. London: Royal Academy of Engineering.

Lucas, B. and Spencer, E. (2016). Written Evidence Submitted by the Centre for Real-World Learning at the University of Winchester and Others. Available at: http://data.parliament.uk/writtenevidence/committeeevidence.svc/evidencedocument/education-committee/purpose-and-quality-of-education-in-england/written/27451.html#_edn42.

Malaguzzi, L. (1998). History, Ideas and Philosophy. In C. Edwards, I. Gandini and G. Foreman (eds), *The Hundred Languages of Children: The Reggio Emilia Approach*. Westport, CT: Ablex Publishing, pp. 49–98.

Marin, L. and Halpern, D. (2011). Pedagogy for Developing Critical Thinking in Adolescents: Explicit Instruction Produces Greatest Gains. *Thinking Skills and Creativity*, 6(1), 1–13.

Marzano, R. (2011). Art & Science of Teaching/What Teachers Gain from Deliberate Practice. *Effective Educator*, 68(4), 82–85. Available at: http://www.ascd.org/publications/educational-leadership/dec10/vol68/num04/What-Teachers-Gain-from-Deliberate-Practice.aspx.

Marzano, R., Pickering, D. and Pollock, J. (2001). *Classroom Instruction That Works: Research-Based Strategies for Increasing Student Achievement*. Alexandria, VA: ASCD.

Ministerial Council on Education, Employment, Training and Youth Affairs (MCEETYA) (2008). *Melbourne Declaration on Educational Goals for Young Australians*. Carlton South, VIC: MCEETYA. Available at: http://www.curriculum.edu.au/verve/_resources/National_Declaration_on_the_Educational_Goals_for_Young_Australians.pdf.

Ofsted (2010). *Learning: Creative Approaches That Raise Standards*. Ref: 080266. Manchester: Ofsted. Available at: http://webarchive.nationalarchives.gov.uk/20141124154759/http://www.ofsted.gov.uk/node/2405.

Ofsted (2011). *Choosing to Volunteer: A Small-Scale Survey to Evaluate the Experiences of Young People Involved in Volunteering in a Range of Settings*. London: Ofsted. Available at: https://www.gov.uk/government/publications/choosing-to-volunteer.

Ofsted (2016). *Getting Ready for Work*. London: Ofsted. Available at: https://www.gov.uk/government/uploads/system/uploads/attachment_data/file/577236/Getting_ready_for_work.pdf.

Organisation for Economic Co-operation and Development (OECD) (2012). *Let's Read Them a Story! The Parent Factor in Education*. Paris: PISA/OECD Publishing. DOI: 10.1787/9789264176232-en

Organisation for Economic Co-operation and Development (OECD) (2013). *PISA 2015: Draft Collaborative Problem Solving Framework*. Paris: OECD Publishing. Available at: https://www.scribd.com/document/149825390/Draft-PISA-2015-Collaborative-Problem-Solving-Framework#download&from_embed.

Organisation for Economic Co-operation and Development (OECD) (2016). *Global Competency for an Inclusive World*. Paris: OECD Publishing. Available at: https://www.oecd.org/education/Global-competency-for-an-inclusive-world.pdf.

Patton, A. (2012). *Work That Matters: The Teacher's Guide to Project-Based Learning*. London: Paul Hamlyn Foundation.

Pennington, B. (2016). Rework Math Problems Daily. *Rochester Institute of Technology/ASC Online* (30 November). Available at: http://www.rit.edu/studentaffairs/asc/online/uncategorized/rework-math-problems-daily/.

Perkins, D. (2009). *Making Learning Whole: How Seven Principles of Teaching Can Transform Education*. San Francisco, CA: Jossey-Bass.

Plucker, J., Beghetto, R. and Dow, G. (2004). Why Isn't Creativity More Important to Educational Psychologists? Potential, Pitfalls, and Future Directions in Creativity Research. *Educational Psychologist*, 39(2), 83–96.

Plucker, J., Kaufman, J. and Beghetto, R. (2015). *What We Know About Creativity*. Washington, DC: Partnership for 21st Century Learning.

Ritchhart, R. (2004). *Intellectual Character: What It Is, Why It Matters, and How to Get It*. San Francisco, CA: Jossey-Bass.

Ritchhart, R., Church, M. and Morrison, K. (2011). *Making Thinking Visible: How to Promote Engagement, Understanding, and Independence for All Learners*. San Francisco, CA: Jossey-Bass.

Robinson, K. (1999). *All Our Futures: Creativity, Culture and Education*. London: Department for Education and Employment.

Robinson, K. (2006). Do Schools Kill Creativity? *TED* [video]. Available at: https://www.ted.com/talks/ken_robinson_says_schools_kill_creativity?language=en.

Robinson, K. (2013). How to Escape Education's Death Valley, *TED*. Available at: https://www.ted.com/talks/ken_robinson_how_to_escape_education_s_death_valley/transcript?language=en.

Robinson, K. and Aronica, L. (2015). *Creative Schools: Revolutionizing Education from the Ground Up*. London: Penguin Random House.

Russell, B. (2016). Bernadette Russell's Top 10 Philosophical Questions Children Should Ask. *The Guardian* (14 February). Available at: https://www.theguardian.com/childrens-books-site/2016/feb/14/philosophical-questions-children-should-ask-bernadette-russell.

References

Schleicher, A. and Tang, Q. (2015). Education Post-2015: Knowledge and Skills Transform Lives and Societies. In E. Hanushek and L. Woessmann (eds), *Universal Basic Skills: What Countries Stand to Gain*. Paris: OECD Publishing, pp. 9–14. DOI: http://dx.doi.org/10.1787/9789264234833-en

Schön, D. (1984). *The Reflective Practitioner: How Professionals Think in Action*. New York: Basic Books.

Sebba, J., Deakin Crick, R., Yu, G., Lawson, H., Harlen, W. and Durant, K. (2008). *Systematic Review of Research Evidence of the Impact on Students in Secondary Schools of Self and Peer Assessment*. London: EPPI-Centre, Institute of Education, University of London. Available at: http://eppi.ioe.ac.uk/cms/Portals/0/PDF%20reviews%20and%20summaries/Self%20Assessment%20report.pdf?ver=2008-10-30-130834-050.

Seligman, M. (2006). *Learned Optimism: How to Change Your Mind and Your Life*. New York: Vintage.

Seligman, M. and Csikszentmihalyi, M. (2000). Positive Psychology: An Introduction. *American Psychologist*, 55(1), 5–14.

Sennett, R. (2008). *The Craftsman*. London: Allen Lane.

Sherrington, T. (2014). The Progressive-Traditional Pedagogy Tree. *Teacherhead* (15 March). Available at: https://teacherhead.com/2014/03/15/the-progressive-traditional-pedagogy-tree/.

Shulman, L. (2005). Signature Pedagogies in the Professions. *Daedalus*, 134(3), 52–59.

Souvignier, E. and Kronenberger, J. (2007). Cooperative Learning in Third Graders' Jigsaw Groups for Mathematics and Science with and without Questioning Training. *British Journal of Educational Psychology*, 77(4), 755–771. DOI: 10.1348/000709906X173297

Sternberg, R. (1996). *Successful Intelligence: How Practical and Creative Intelligence Determine Success in Life*. New York: Simon & Schuster.

Stoll, L. and Temperley, J. (2009). Creative Leadership: A Challenge of Our Times. *School Leadership and Management*, 29(1), 63–76.

Tidemann, A. and Ozturk, P. (2008). Learning Dance Movements by Imitation: A Multiple Model Approach. In A. Dengel, K. Berns, T. M. Breuel, F. Bomarius and T. R. Roth-Berghofer (eds), *KI 2008: Advances in Artificial Intelligence. Proceedings of the 31st Annual German Conference on AI, KI 2008, Kaiserslautern, Germany, September 23–26, 2008*. Berlin and Heidelberg: Springer-Verlag, pp. 380–388.

Torrance, E. P. (1970). *Encouraging Creativity in the Classroom*. Dubuque, IA: William C. Brown.

Treffinger, D., Young, G., Selby, E. and Shepardson, C. (2002). *Assessing Creativity: A Guide for Educators*. Storrs, CT: National Research Centre on the Gifted and Talented.

Vincent-Lancrin, S. (2013). Creativity in Schools: What Countries Do (Or Could Do). *Education Week* (11 April). Available at: http://blogs.edweek.org/edweek/global_learning/2013/04/creativity_in_schools_what_countries_do_or_could_do.html.

Waters, L., Barsky, A., Ridd, A. and Allen, K. (2015). Contemplative Education: A Systematic, Evidence-Based Review of the Effect of Meditation Interventions in Schools. *Educational Psychology Review*, 27(1), 103–134.

Watkins, C. (2005). *Classrooms as Learning Communities: What's In It for Schools?* Abingdon: Routledge.

Watson, D., Nordin-Bates, S. and Chappell, K. (2012). Facilitating and Nurturing Creativity in Pre-Vocational Dancers: Findings from the UK Centres for Advanced Training. *Research in Dance Education*, 13(2), 153–173.

Wiliam, D. (2006). Assessment for Learning: Why, What and How. Keynote speech delivered at the Cambridge Assessment Network Conference, Faculty of Education, University of Cambridge, 15 September. Available at: http://www.dylanwiliam.org/Dylan_Wiliams_website/Papers.html.

Woolf, V. (2012). *A Writer's Diary: Being Extracts from the Diary of Virginia Woolf.* New York: Houghton Mifflin Harcourt.

World Economic Forum (2016). *The Future of Jobs: Employment, Skills and Workforce Strategy for the Fourth Industrial Revolution. Global Challenge Insight Report.* Geneva: World Economic Forum. Available at: http://www3.weforum.org/docs/WEF_Future_of_Jobs.pdf.